Voices Still Heard, Dreams Still Believed, Scenes Still Viewed

DORIS EZELL-SCHMITZ

ISBN 978-1-64079-912-7 (paperback)
ISBN 978-1-64079-913-4 (digital)

Christian Faith Publishing, Inc.
832 Park Avenue
Meadville, PA 16335
www.christianfaithpublishing.com

Printed in the United States of America

Contents

To Madelyn and Eloise, Ezra, who will one day pick up a book to read, and to MacKenzie, Alex, and Braxton, who have long since picked up books and read them.

It is my hope, my wish, that all of you will pick up this book and read it with the same passion and vigor that was put into the writing of it, *Voices Still Heard, Dreams Still Believed, Scenes Still Viewed.*

The content of this book is true, but the names have been changed to protect the characters' true identities, with the exception of my sister, Vera, my friend, Anna Lee, my mother, my grandmother and me, Doris.

Introduction

A FRIEND TOLD ME, "YOU TALK about the past too much. It's like you're living in it. I live in the present, in the future."

I thought about it for the longest. Why not? My memories are there, way back there—memories of the children I once knew, what we did, how we lived and played, what we said, even what we wore. I remembered faces, names, whose brother or sister belonged to whom. I had memories of where I went, whether by myself, with my sister, with my mother, grandmother, or with a friend.

I remembered the classes I had and the teachers who taught them. Whether they were nice or strict or downright mean: did they whip, make you stand in the corner holding a stack of books, heavy books, dictionaries at that, plus called your mother and sent her a note that had better get delivered.

I remembered the cute boys (cousins) who moved to my school, Edgefield Elementary, and the one who stole my sixth-grade heart, who did The Twist with me at our spring dance, who made all A's and saw me with my hair all fluffy and hanging loose around my shoulders, who saw me in my fancy dress; only who stayed through spring but who was gone the next year.

I had the sweet memory of our neighbor's German Shepherd, Dash, who loved Anna Lee and me, and who lived under the cruelty of his owner who beat him mercilessly, for no reason, every day. We could hear the licks up and down our street.

What more is there but memory to fall upon? So that's where the people and the events, the good times and not so good times, and the freedoms of our growing up meet, intermingle, and depart, making room for more reality to transpire.

I will always reach back through the years feeling the hands that lifted me up when I fell and skinned my knee—I had cried, not because my knee was hurt but my pride.

Oh, yes, I would look back and keep looking back—there might be someone still standing in the shadows who thinks she's not cute or not cute enough. Girls can be so mean.

I would look back through in time to feel that navy purple pain of the leg that broke when I fell, to see the bully who had dared talk about my mother and grandmother, who had gotten the beating of her eleven years of life, of the brothers who came one Sunday afternoon, begging for food—they were hungry.

I remembered my tenth birthday party when we six girls played games, ate cake, and did the Twist, my doll Donna that Mama gave away.

I remembered so much more, so many more people. Oh, yes, I will continue to go back in time to the past. It's where I keep my best material.

The memories made on Miller Street when I was growing up are a mixture of wonder-filled and bittersweet wrapped into one. They have been there, nesting the new sun waiting to rise on another day. What adventure awaited me, I would often ask myself when I got up in the morning.

A friend said that I dwell too much in the past, that I should focus on the present and the future. She wondered why. My only reason was that there is no story in the present and the future. The past takes me back to the children I played with, loved, fought with, the dog that followed me around and licked my face, the taste of those awful grits, which I hated, inside my mouth on those cold winter mornings.

What story can be derived from the now, from the what-will-happen-when-tomorrow finally comes? The answer has got to be none.

So yes, it's back, back, way back, to the past I go to hear voices once stilled, believe dreams once lost, and view scenes once forgotten.

The Conversation

CARL WAS WATCHING ME WHILE I was watching him watching me, but neither of us acknowledged this detail. We only dismissed it as something sixth-grade boys and girls who were supposed to be boyfriend and girlfriend to do. Nothing more.

In class, all we could do was wait for the bell when we could walk beside each other to the buses, though we rode different ones. We could talk briefly on the way.

"Are you watching TV tonight?" I'd ask.

"If I'm finished my paper route," he'd answer.

"How long have you had it?" I'd ask, just to have something else to say.

"A year," he'd tell me, something I already knew.

"Is it fun?" I'd ask next.

"No. But it lets me make money," he'd say.

"Yeah," I'd say, then would hush because I wouldn't have anything else to say. Plus, we'd be at the bus lot by then, no more time to say anything else if we did have something else to say.

"Will you call me tonight, Carl?" I got up the nerve to ask. He stopped, grinning like a Cheshire Cat.

"Okay, if my mom lets me. I've still got your number, if it's the same," he said.

"Okay. It's the same," I assured him.

We parted ways, grinning widely. I hoped his mother would let him use that phone. He'd better make it before 7:30, when that black phone was put to bed, by Mama's rule.

That evening, Sister and I were watching *Amos and Andy* on our black-and-white TV set when the phone rang.

"I'll get it," I offered.

"You better let Mama or Mother get it, Doris. It's probably for one of them anyway," Sister told me. Sister. She seemed always right about things. But not this time.

"No, Sister, I'll get it!" I told her. "If it's for one of them, I'll just get 'em!"

I spoke into the receiver.

"Hello. Ezell's residence. May I help you?" I said, trying to sound grown-up.

"Hi, Doris. This is Carl. I did my homework. It was easy. Did you do yours?"

He barely gave me anytime to respond. But I didn't care. What mattered was that he had called—really, really called. Carl was on the other end of the receiver, actually making conversation with me. His mother must have given him permission to call me. Or maybe he'd sneaked and called. No, he'd never do that. He would never be mischievous.

"Carl," I blubbered, "are we gonna walk beside each tomorrow like we did today? You know, when we walked out to our buses?"

"Yeah, Doris, probably we will. We'll probably do that all the time now," he said.

"Really, Carl?"

"Really, Doris," he answered, sounding like a declaration rather than a promise. "Well, Doris, I know you've got to do your homework. The English is easy, but the arithmetic is hard," Carl warned.

"Okay, Carl. Thanks. I'm doing the arithmetic first, to get it out the way. I love English, though. It's fun, kind of," I put in, laughing, though there was absolutely nothing funny.

My laugh must have been a bit too loud, for Mama spun into quick view right then and there.

"Get off the phone, Doris, and get your lessons done!" she puffed, getting louder with each word she spoke.

I heard Carl chuckle.

"See you in the morning, Doris."

"Yeah. Goo-dbye, Carl," I said in my dreamiest voice, putting the pone on the hooks.

I eased by Mama and went off to complete my homework. Grinning from one ear to the other, I knew I'd have no trouble falling asleep tonight.

The Cause to Giggle

I CAN'T REALLY REMEMBER WHICH ONE of us girls was the first one to giggle or who suddenly stopped the laughter. It could have Rose, who sat at the front of our pew, dressed in a pink and white lacy wide-tail dress with a crinoline slip underneath. It was a pretty dress, only she wore it every other Sunday. By now everyone had to know it was her last year's Easter dress.

Perhaps Nora was the first to giggle. She was sitting right beside Rose and was dressed in a pale green skirt, pleated, with a green and white checkered top. Over it was a white jacket trimmed in green. Nora had a sly expression on her face that would make her look guilty, even if she were not.

Then there was Kim, the new girl who had just moved with her family from another church in town. Surely she wouldn't be brave enough to giggle outright. Or would she? I really didn't think so.

Pam who was sitting beside me tapped me on the shoulder.

"Doris, who do you think was doing all that giggling? Rose, Nora, or Kim? It couldn't have been you. And it surely wasn't me," Pam said with question marks in her voice and on her face.

"Gee, Pam, I wonder, too. Somebody's going to be in big-time trouble if Mama Lee finds out. She knows all of our mothers, and she will get a kick out of telling."

"I'll get the blame. I'll just betcha they'll blame it on me. If Mother asks about the giggling, will you stick up for me, Pam? After all, I wasn't in it. It came from that end of the pew, not ours, right?" I said, defending myself.

"Right. But—" Pam stopped, seemingly at a loss for words, which was quite unusual for her.

The giggling occurred again. This time the whole row of us had our white-gloved hands over our mouths, trying to bury our laughter which was opening surfing.

By the time the preacher appeared in the pulpit, Mama had seated herself in our pew, positioning herself right in the middle of us girls, bringing the giggling to a complete, sudden stop, unannounced to say the least.

Party Girls from Two to Four

W HEN I WAS NINE, AFTER talking, Mama and Mother had made a grand declaration: "You may have a party. After all, you'll be ten, baby!" Mother had chuckled, like this was big news.

"Oh, boy! Oh, boy!" I jumped up in the air, celebrating already. "I'll write out my list after lunch."

"Now, not too many children." Mama cautioned. "Can't have children coming in here, messing everything up."

"Yes, m'am." I gulped lunch down, not even tasting the tuna sandwich, cookie, and glass of milk. I was so excited.

My first list had ten names on it. I gave it to the women who waited in the living room. They passed it from person, each perusing it, each shaking her head *no*.

"Take off some names, Doris. Get your list down some, say down, to oh, five girls," Mother suggested.

I huffed, knowing it was only in vain. I had to do what they said, or no party at all.

So I took the list, looked it over, made my decision, and scratched out five names, my friends. I handed it back to Mother.

"On my way from school tomorrow, I can pick up invitations. Or would you rather pick them out yourself? After all, it *is* your party," Mother offered, almost singing.

"Oh, you can get them. It'll be fine whatever you get. And thanks!" I hugged her hard.

That night after dinner and homework, Mother and I sat at the dining room table, talking softly for about twenty minutes about the party.

"Let's see, Doris, we need party hats, five. Blow outs, five. Poppers, five, and a cake and ten candles. What color do you want?" she paused.

Gleefully I chirped, "Pink! I want pink roses and green leaves with pink trim. I just love birthday cake!"

"Child, how are you paying for this?" she questioned, smiling, laughing. "You sure better hurry up and call De-troit!" When she split the words up, I knew to take cover. She was hot, on fire, ready to burn up.

"Will you take me with you to Betty's Cake Box to order? Maybe we can get some brownies there?" I asked, picking up the party list.

"No brownies, child. You want your teeth to rot out?"

"No, m'am, but I love brownies."

"People downstairs love ice water too. Make sure that home-work's finished. Take your bath, then get to bed!"

"Yes, m'am!"

I did as Mother asked, but before I hopped in bed, I went over my birthday party list. Yes, five names were on it—my friends, my pals—girls I laughed with, cried with, or got mad at, but in the next one or two minutes, I was friends with them again. The squabbles we had didn't last; in fact, after they were over, we'd wonder why we squabbled in the first place.

There was Katie, whom I'd met one Sunday. We were at the water fountain, drinking the water at first, then we'd started playfully flicking it at each other.

I'd met Patty in church too, her sitting beside me in Sunday school. We were playing with the nickel she had to put in the collection plate.

Ruthie was already ten, and we'd been friends for years. She was quiet and didn't like to talk much. I'd never seen her dance.

Brenda and Linda, the identical twins, had met me because their mother worked with mine. I found out later that Brenda would come to my party, but Linda would not. (She would be out of town.) And though she made six, Anna Lee was on my list.

With the invitations filled out in my best script and mailed, I grew more excited, especially in a matter of days they'd all called to say they were coming.

The special day arrived with a blazing March sun. Beaming Saturdays were always fun, but this particular Saturday would be more than fun. As I waited for my friends and the cake, I thought about last year's party, and the two boys who had come: Randy Deerfield, who'd tried to peep under our dresses, and Lonnie Sawyer who'd cried because he couldn't take his present back home with him.

The doorbell chimed twice on the side door. I leaped up from the couch and answered it, my crinoline rustling. It was Ruthie, smiling and holding a small box wrapped in blue paper. "Hi, Ruthie, I'm glad you came! Come on in and have a seat. I like your dress," I told her. We went to the couch.

"Thanks, and here's your present. I hope you like it," she added hopefully.

"I'll put it on the bed," I told her as the front doorbell sounded, its four gongs sounding.

"Ruthie, can you get that?" I asked, putting her present on the guest bed. It was Katie. She told me this, calling from the door. She took her over to the couch and put the present on the bed.

Anna Lee and Patty, the last to come, ringing the back door bell, one *gong, ding*. I skipped to the door where they stood smiling and holding out their presents. "Your dresses are so pretty," I told them both. "Come on in, Anna Lee and Patty! I'm so glad you came," I chortled. "We're all on the couch right now," I informed them, as I took their presents wrapped in pink paper. They joined the small crowd while I put the presents on the bed with the others.

Mother came through, urging us to go outside; we were beginning to got on her nerves, I felt, so I spoke up, "Hey, let's go outside and play!"

"Okay!" they all echoed in one voice. We piled out through the front door, our crinolines making their own noise, like a song.

We played a ring game Little Sally Walker. I loved this game because you acted out the parts to the lyrics. You sat in the saucer, you rose, you put your hands on your hips, you let your backbone slip, you shook it to the east, you shook it to the west. Lastly, you shook it to the one that you loved the best.

We played Hop Scotch, One, Two, Three, Red Light, and Posing. After a hearty game of See-saw, See-saw, we went back inside, and I asked Mother if she'd cut on the record player. She did and put on "The Twist."

Before long, the coffee table was pulled back, making dancing room. The party attendees cut loose, twisting on the living room rug. We sang along with Chubby Checker, off key as we could be, but knowing all his words.

We twisted and sang along with Chubby, "Come on, baby, and let's do the Twist. Come on baby, and let's do the Twist! Take me by your little hand and go like this!" We girls were still twisting when both Mama and Mother came in and let us know cake time had come.

"Come on, girls." Mother smiled firmly. "Or I'm gonna eat it all by myself!" Mama added. We giggled, heading into the dining room. There were hot dogs with chili, mustard and ketchup, chocolate chip cookies, Wise potato chips, and punch in party cups.

The cake from Betty's Cake Box sat in the middle of the table. The ten pink candles had been perfectly placed and waited for someone to light their wicks. That someone was Mother, who knew this was her duty. She bent over the cake; someone squealed. We all giggled, waiting for the sweet treat to grace our mouths. "Now, girls, let's sing Happy Birthday." She led, and they followed.

"Happy birthday to you, happy birthday to you, happy birthday, dear Doris, happy birthday to you!" They sang the other verses, and when they get to "How old are you? How old are you? How old are you? How old are you?" I responded happily, "I'm ten years old! I'm ten years old! I'm ten years old! I'm ten years old!" The song ended with them singing, "We love you, we do! We love you, we do! We love you, dear Doris! We love you, we do!"

Doris blowing out birthday candles

We were having so much fun! We were just being little girls try-ing to grow up. Innocent, cute, pretty, smart. Not yet knowing that there were bad people out there who would get us if they could. But that would never happen, would it? Could it?

"Doris," Mother urged tenderly, "time to make your wish and *blow* out the candles."

"Yes, m'am." I thought for just a moment, leaned over, took a big whiff of air, and blew with all my might. Like magic, all ten burn-ing candles—*out!* My wish for a boyfriend, for all A's on my report card, for a pony or a dog would certainly come true, in time.

As Mother took the smoking candles off the cake and sliced off big pieces of cake, we girls ate our hot dogs while eyeing the slices being put on our napkins. We chewed and licked our lips as we waited for birthday cake. We had no worries, no cares, nothing to worry about. "This is so good," declared Patty, putting cake into her mouth.

"Patty," Anna Lee interjected, "Mrs. Garner said don't talk with food in your mouth!"

"Yeah, but Mrs. Garner isn't here." We all laughed. Mrs. Garner had once been our Sunday School teacher. She was nice. She had two kids, Raymond and Katy. One weekend in the summer, Mrs. Garner had gone away with just her and Mr. Garner. She never came back. They had found her, though, one week later, floating in a nearby lake. (I'd heard Mama and Ms. Harris talking about it on the back porch.)

We finished our food, full and happy. Time to open presents. We bounded into the guest bedroom where each present sat on the freshly made fluffy pink bedspread.

"Open mine first," someone squeaked. I couldn't tell who. "No, mine."

"Mine!"

"Mine!"

"Open mine!"

We were all laughing, not getting anything done, I mean anything done. Mother *and* Mama were in the room now to see what *all* was going on. "What's so funny? I want to laugh, too!" Mother grinned at us, seemingly sensing what was happening.

"Tell you what," she suggested, "let's let the birthday girl pick the present to be opened, okay?" We shook our heads in unison, feeling defeated. Mother knows best. Patty had brought me a Bingo game; Anna Lee, a Chinese Checkers set; Katie had brought a slip, some socks and panties. Linda had brought a burette set and some hair bows and ribbons, and Ruthie had brought a Tiny Tears doll. (She could cry real tears.)

After the presents had been opened, we sat on the couch and watched *Leave it to Beaver* while waiting for the mothers to pick up their girls. We kicked our legs, displaying our best lace-trimmed, white socks. I couldn't help but think what fun this day, this whole afternoon, had been; I couldn't help thinking how pretty everybody looked in their fancy party dresses and white Sunday socks. What a day this had been. And there was leftover cake. We'd be eating into next week even.

When Sister came home, I was out of breath, happily telling her about each thing that had happened—each girl who had come, each present she had brought. I went on and on, following her from one room to the next room. I talked so much, laughing at times, slowing down at other times.

I was just getting ready to repeat myself, for I'd already told her about when the girls sang Happy Birthday, when I stopped to see Mama standing in the middle of the kitchen floor, glaring over her glasses, throwing me that look.

I knew I should hush my mouth; after all, I had been warned. But I was still so excited, so pumped up that I kept right on giving Sister the highlights of my party. "And, Sister," I offered, "when I blew out my candles, I got 'em out on my very first try. My very first try! We did The Twist, played Little Sally Walker and One, Two, Three, Red Light! We had the best time, Sister! Come see my presents." I took her hand and led her into the guest bedroom where my treasures were displayed on the bed. Sister and I stood at the edge of the bed, with her admiring each treasure.

"You surely got some nice things, Doris. We can play Bingo and Chinese Checkers now," she told me.

I laughed and shook my head in agreement. "Are you going to have a party when your birthday comes?" I asked her.

"Probably."

"Wouldn't it be good if we had birthdays every day?" I asked, closing my eyes to sleep.

She didn't answer that one. I think she was already sleeping.

Delores, Our Weekend Guest

MARCH HAD BEEN COLD THAT year when I was nine. It had blown in snow after snow. One blanket would melt down; another would form, sometimes in the night, sometimes during the day. If it came during day, we'd get out of school early.

I remember how Mrs. Sawyer's car would go trudging through the slush that was already on the road. I'd watch the buses rumble by, taking my friends to another part of town. I wondered who would be waiting for them. I knew too well who'd be at my back door when Mr. Sawyer let me out—Mama, smiling, a saucer of cookies in one hand, a glass of milk in the other.

She first smiled like she was glad I was home. She asked, "How was my baby's day?" She reached out the saucer.

"Let me take off my coat." I laughed.

"Oh, that's right!" She put the saucer and glass down and helped me out of my coat, scarf, and galoshes, which I hated.

"I made ninety on my spelling test!" I told her happily, biting into the warm chocolate cookie.

"That's good, baby. Next time, you'll make one hundred."

That was Mama—never ever satisfied, always wanting me to be at the next highest level. Now Mother would have been glad over my good mark.

Before we knew it, March was gone, leaving only its memory of the snows it had born. April skipped in on bright sunbeams in daytime, and glowing full moons teamed up with glittering stars at night.

I remember when the telephone had rung. It was the operator with a long-distance call. Trying hard to hear what was being said, but realizing I couldn't, simply made me wait impatiently.

Finally, Mother hung up the phone. She came into the hallway, smiling. "Girls, that was Mrs. Jeffers, Delores's mother. Easter weekend, she's going out of town, and she's letting Delores stay with us."

I clapped my hands and jumped up. I liked this girl. "Mother," I inquired, "is she gonna bring a suitcase?"

Mother, Sister, and Mama all stared at me with question marks in their eyes. "How else would she get her stuff up here?" they all seemed to ask.

It was Sister who dared to ponder, saying, "What else do you think she'd use for her things? A brown paper sack?"

"Oh!" It's all I could think of saying.

"We'll pick her up after we all get from school, the Thursday before Good Friday. And I'm warning you right now. Be on your best behavior," she had said to both of us, but I knew she meant it for me.

Thursday afternoon, the four of us loaded into the '59 Fairlane Ford. Mother worshipped that car; Mama had once told Mrs. Harris, one of her friends.

On the ride to Chess Town, Sister and I played a game where we claimed everything on the right of the road was hers, and everything on the left side was mine. The winner was whoever had the most or the biggest. Sister had won. "I'll win going back!" I laughed.

When we got to Delores's house, she was standing on the porch. Beside her was a red suitcase. I started to get out, but Mama looked back, giving me the eye. Mother got out first. Delores's mother came out on the porch and stood beside Delores; they looked like each other. Both were smiling.

Mama got out, followed by Sister, followed by me. We were suddenly all talking at the same time excitedly, getting out of breath. Delores had a doll in her right arm and a stuffed poodle dog in her left. "Oh, boy," I thought to myself, "she still likes toys." Most of my friends thought they were too old to play with them, except, of course, Anna Lee.

"Delores, we're gonna have so much fun." I panted at the same she was asking, "Am I going to sleep in your bed?"

"Guess what!" I chortled. She jerked around, looking straight into my eyes. We were the exact same height. "We're having pancakes in the morning when we get up. Mama makes them so good!" I licked my lips. She was grinning widely, delighted.

Mother put her suitcase in the trunk; then we piled into the car. Mrs. Jeffers leaned over in, bending into the window.

"Lois," she lectured sternly, strict, "I've already told you whatever Nellie and Mrs. Lowry tell you to do, you'd better hop and do it. I'd better get a number one good report from both of them when they bring you back. You hear me, I hope. Nellie, you've got my number. Lois doesn't want to hear my voice on that phone. Do you, Lois?" she added, looking at her daughter.

"Oh, no, m'am, Mommy. I know how to act." She grinned. "I promise to be good and mind." She blew her mother a kiss.

"Well," Mother said finally, "she'll be fine. We're happy to have her. We'll see you on Monday about this same time. Be sure to tell your husband hello for us."

We all waved as Mother backed out into the street. "So, Delores, what grade are you this year? Sixth? Same as Doris?" Mother pondered.

"Yes, m'am." She laughed. "Mommy says I'm getting old."

"Are you looking forward to the seventh grade?" she continued. Why was she talking to Delores? She was my friend, not hers, after all.

"Yes, m'am, I am," Delores answered, trying to be polite. I guess her mother had schooled her well. "I've heard the subjects are hard, though, in seventh grade," Delores said.

"They aren't really," Sister told her, trying to sound knowledgeable. "Science and math are a bit harder, but English and health are just about the same. You still have to conjugate verbs and diagram sentences. Health, safety, and hygiene are the exact same. Nothing changes except the pictures."

"That helps some, Vera." Delores promised. "Or do you want me to call you 'Sister' like Doris does?"

25

"Vera is fine, or Sister, either one. Vera makes me feel grown up, but Sister is just fine too."

"I know," Delores suggested, "I'll call you Sister Vera! Okay?" She giggled, proud of her idea.

"Okay by me," Sister grimed.

"You can call me Dot-T," I told her, using what Daddy had called me one time on the phone.

We played the same *What's Mine?* traveling back home. This time, I won. Delores was on my team. She seemed to have liked the game as much as Sister and I did.

We were home before we knew it. Mother took Delores's suitcase out. She laughed. "Did you pack bricks instead of clothes? Or are your shoes just that heavy?"

"Oh, Mrs. Ezell," Delores chirped, hopping over me and out of the car. "Don't bother yourself. I can carry that suitcase. It's not that heavy, and Doris can help me!"

"Thanks a lot, Delores, for volunteering your friend, I think, but keep quiet."

Mama broke in. "I bet you three are hungry!"

All three of us, sounding like hens cackling, admitted, "Yes, m'am!"

"I could eat a whole cow," I said.

"I could eat a horse," Delores said.

"I could eat my leg!" Sister said.

We burst out laughing.

"No cows, horses, or legs on the menu today. Try back tomorrow for that. Now, what I do have? How about hot dogs with chili, mustard, ketchup and onions, baked beans, and Coca-Cola?"

"That sounds so good, Mrs. Lowry. Thank you. Do you want us to help you?" Delores said politely.

"You girls may set the table, get the napkins ready, put them on the dining room table, and wash your hands," Mama told us.

"Boy, I think, *was she belting out the commands!*"

"Mrs. Lowry," Delores whispered to Mama, "I don't care for onions on my hot dog."

Mama was fixing the hot dogs, piling on everything to make them all the way.

She smiled at Delores, saying, "Aw, baby, you don't have to have onions. I like them, but they don't like me. Every time I try to eat onions, I get heartburn."

"These hot dogs were so good. So were the baked beans," I told Mama. And we're having vanilla ice cream for dessert. *It can't get better*, I thought.

"Girls," Mama told us as we finished up, "if you're finished eating, you can clear the table and get the dishes done, all three of you."

"Yes, m'am," we chirped altogether. Delores was one of us. She wasn't getting out of anything.

"I thought we were getting ice cream," I grumbled, daring to poke my lips out. I stopped abruptly when Mama called, "Girls, get to work! You *do* want ice cream!" Her exclamation was more like a question that needed no answer. Boy, but did we work, and fast.

"We've finished, Mama!" Sister called, proud of our teamwork. Mama came in, her apron on, and inspected what we'd done. She went over everything, and when she was satisfied, she dismissed her young workers, smiling and nodding her head. "Now you can have ice cream," she laughed. "You girls are ready to go to Mr. Rob's."

Mr. Rob's was the hot dog place where all of the colored people went on Saturdays for lunch. Sometimes, if Mama had a babysitting job, Mother would take Sister and me. We loved it.

The three of us watched as Mama scooped up vanilla ice cream and put it in a bowl or on cones, whichever we chose. My, my, we almost couldn't wait. "Hurry, Mama!" I thought, only smiling, daring not to say one word, realizing the ice cream *was* hard. It had been in the frig for a while.

Delores and I got cones; Sister got a bowl. She didn't want it getting on her fingers. I didn't care. What was licking made for, anyway?

We ate and slurped, slurped, and licked. It was so good. We got full, but we didn't stop. I licked my fingers, stopping only when Sister chided, "Doris, aren't you ashamed? Use a napkin." I wanted to tell her to shut her face, but I used my common sense and got a napkin. As always, Sister knew best.

Full of ice cream and happy, happy, we were back home and ready to watch TV. *I Love Lucy* was already on. Delores and I sat on the floor, Sister on the couch.

Too soon, I thought, Mother came in, cut the TV off—right when *Rawhide* was coming on, and we could see that cute Rowdy Yates—and announced, "Bath time, girls. You can take bubble baths. Delores, you go first. You're our guest."

When Mother went back out, I jumped up and said, "I know, we can all get in the tub together. It will go faster that way, and we'll have a little more time to play."

Sister and Delores looked puzzled, probably thinking, *Okay*. But they were nervous; I could tell they were. To tell the truth, so was I.

Mother had filled the tub with water just right; it wasn't too hot, and it wasn't too cold. She'd poured in the bubble stuff, already making big and little bubbles.

Stripped down with nothing on, we got in the tub, Delores first, who said, "Y'all sure is this going to work?"

"Sister and I take baths together all the time," I puffed, "what's one more person in the tub?"

So Sister got in, then me. We splashed around, put bubbles in each other's faces, and did all except use the bath cloths Mother had put out. We tickled each other, giggling, which our folks must have heard. Because before long, the door opened and there stood Mama, looking like, as she always told her friend, "just about like trees walking."

Our mouths dropped open, but no sound, no words came out. We just looked at her, waiting, but I didn't know what we were waiting for. I thought about that strap hanging up in the closet and the last time she'd used it on me. I had gone to the Rec with my friend Linda and hadn't come home on time. I'd cried and cried and promised I wouldn't do it again. I'd had welts for days from where she had used it, and Sister had teased, "Doris, you will never learn, will you?" That's when I'd said my first cuss word, telling her where she should and could go. Mama came in and grabbed Delores's bath cloth, surprising us all when she washed and scrubbed her face and body.

"Now, up you go and dry yourself off. real well. Can't have you catching a cold." Delores did as she was told, with not a word back.

Mama did the same to Sister and me and had us all to brush our teeth after we'd put on our pajamas.

"I like your pajamas," I told Delores. "Could we swap tomorrow night?"

"That might not be a good idea. Mrs. Lowry might get mad," she said.

"Mama's gonna be babysitting tomorrow when we take our baths."

Sister was taking it all in. "Yeah," she chimed in, "that's true. But remember, Mother's gonna be here, and she's not that strict. Why—"

I was going to say more, but Sister interrupted, saying, "Doris, why do you love trouble?"

So it was settled: I'd sleep in my own pajamas.

"Yes, m'am, Mrs. Lowry, anytime you want another granddaughter, I'm yours." She laughed.

"You've got all of our words," Mama responded, hugging her. We were all sitting around the dining room table.

"Boy," I thought, "was I going to miss that girl when she left."

"Mama, are you ever going to learn how to drive?" Sister asked.

"No, honey, I drive Buck and Bill, my two feet. I was driving with your daddy once, and he hollered at me. That made me lose my nerve, and I've never tried anymore."

"Did you use to like school when you were little?" I asked her.

"Oh, yes, I did, but we only went to school four months out of the year. The other months, we worked on the farm, planting cotton, hoeing it, and picking it. My daddy couldn't read or write, and he signed his name with a capital X. He loved God, and he'd get Babe or me to read the *Bible* to him every night. He loved his family. We didn't have much, but there was a lot of love in that house."

"Did you ride the bus to school?" Delores asked.

"No, no, honey," Mama told her/us. "We had to walk three miles one way in the rain and snow. We'd see the bus pass by carrying the white children to their school that was about four miles from ours. They'd look at us, but our folks had warned us not to look at white folks." She stopped and breathed hard. "Times have really changed," she sighed.

"Mama, would you get anything for Christmas? And how did you spend Christmas?" I asked her.

"Oh, we'd get something like a horn for the boys. And the girls would sometimes get dolls made out of corn shucks. We'd go to church for a sermon and singing. Sometimes after church, there'd be a party. People would have big kettles of food. We'd dance and everything. It was fun times, fun times."

"Wow," was all I could say.

"How many brothers and sisters did you have, Mama?" Sister asked.

"Eight. Four brothers and four sisters. There were Sam, Josh, Buddin, Paul, Elizabeth or Babe, Kate, Henrietta, and Joyce. All of them were dead except Babe, Kate, and Josh. You saw Lizzie—we call her Babe—the other day out in the country. She's the one who wrung the chickens' necks. Remember?"

"Yes, m'am," Delores laughed. "I'll never forget that scene. The chickens with no heads flopping around on the ground, getting blood all over."

"Yeah," Sister said, "that sure enough was something else."

"Oh, I had the best time this weekend!" Delores chirped, sounding just like a bird.

"Do you have a boyfriend?" I asked Delores.

"No, at least not a real one. There's this one boy in class I think is kinda cute. I think he likes me. He's always looking at me anyway," she told us, trying to keep her voice low.

"Is he cute?" I whispered. We all giggled. Delores turned colors and grinned, "Yeah, he's *real* cute!" We burst out laughing.

Mother turned onto Baker Street, where Delores's house was. We turned into their driveway. Her mommy was peering out the window.

The car stopped, and we all bailed out. "Well, hello, stranger!" her mommy said, smiling. "You know, I think you've grown some since you've been gone."

"I probably have, with all of Mrs. Lowry's good cooking filling me up all the time," Delores laughed. "The best food all the time!"

Mama was trying hard not to smile, but she was loving Delores's words, I could tell.

"Honey, don't I know it! Mrs. Lowry can burn. Always been like that. And Nellie Mae ain't too bad herself. So I know you've had a good time at that table."

"We really enjoyed having her. Let her come back," Mother urged.

"We'll talk about it more for the summer," Mrs. Jeffers said. "Maybe yours can come down here for a while."

"Oh boy!" I shouted.

"It's not summer yet, Doris," Mother reminded me. "And besides, you're still in sixth grade."

We all hugged each other, said our good-byes, and started out to the car. Sister and I slowly got into the back. We were quiet. Mama and Mother got in; they too were quiet.

"We'll have to send Delores a picture of the three of us," I said as we backed out into the street. We were all still waving as Mother drove on to the next street.

"Yes, we will," Mother said. "The pictures should be ready by tomorrow, at least. I had some extra prints made, and I'll drop some in the mail when I pick them up. You had quite the weekend, didn't you?"

"We sure did," I admitted. "Delores is a real nice girl and a good friend too."

"Mama," I said, "may I have a piece of coconut cake when we get home?"

"You don't need more cake, girl!" she responded.

"Doris!" Mama laughed. Sister too, I didn't think. I looked up at her, grinning. "I want a ponytail that bounces up and down!" I yelped.

Mother looked at me, smiled, and simply said, "I can fix you a ponytail but can't promise it'll bounce up and down."

"That's close enough!"

Mother combed and pulled and brushed and smoothed my hair until most of the tangles were gone. She put more Vaseline on until all the naps had left. Then she brushed the hair up from the back, hurting when a nap caught in the kitchen.

"Ouch!" I screamed. "That hurt!"

Mother only ignored me and twisted a green rubber band around my hair. She pulled it tight.

"That hurts!" I screeched.

"Oh, Doris, hush," she warned me. "You're okay. You're a big girl."

"Yeah," I added, "but big girls can hurt." She only laughed and gathered the comb, brush, grease, and towel to put them away.

I looked in the full-length mirror at my ponytail and shook it. It didn't bounce. Maybe I shook it wrong. But what other way was there to shake it but the way I had before? I tried it again. No bounce.

I'd have to ask Delores about it. She'd know. Mother ran her fingers through my ponytail.

"Ow!" she put her hand on mine.

"Too much Vaseline," she said, rubbing her greasy hand against mine.

"Will it ever bounce up and down like yours?"

"Keep the grease out and yes. You'll have a bouncy ball ponytail, just like mine," she promised. Now, how to tell Mother who swore by Vaseline.

"Would you girls like some cake and milk before we leave?" Mama asked us. It was about twelve when we'd normally eat lunch. Cake and milk sounded great. We all shook our heads yes. Even Mother got a slice. Mama surely could bake good cakes.

We girls ate slowly, trying to prolong the time we had left. Mother had called Delores's mommy to let her know we were coming.

"I really had a good time y'all," Delores said as we walked out of the kitchen.

"Yeah," I responded, "we had some real fun."

"We sure did," Sister agreed, grinning. "You girls make the bed?" Mama asked, putting the dishes in the sink. "You want to wash them now or when we get back?"

"Now!" We all answered in one big voice. More time with Delores if we did them now. We really took our time washing, then drying, then putting away. It was the first time I'd had fun doing a task. I hoped it would continue.

We sang "Here Comes Peter Cotton Tail" and "The Easter Parade." We sounded pretty awful, but it was still fun.

Mother came into the kitchen. "Okay, young ladies, time to get a move on." The three of us walked toward the back to Sister and my room to get Delores's suitcase.

"Delores," Mama beamed, coming out of her room, "it's been a joy having you. You will come back to see us?"

Delores would sleep in hers.

We put on our hairnets and said our prayers and got into bed. Delores was in the middle, Sister was on the outside—one wrong move, and she was on the floor—I was on the side closest to the wall.

Mama and Mother came in, and one by one they patted our heads and kissed our cheeks.

"Do you remember to say your prayers?" Mama asked.

"Oh, yes, m'am. We couldn't forget our prayers," Sister purred, sounding like that big yellow cat who lived down the street.

"Now, you girls go right to sleep. No playing around, you hear?"

"Yes, m'am," we said together, not meaning a word, for as soon as they were out, we started playing Turning Heads, giggling wildly. One time, Sister bumped Delores in the head.

"Aw," she howled. "That hurt!"

"Sorry," Sister chimed. I couldn't hold my laughter in.

Mama and Mother were back in our room, Mama holding her black belt.

All I could think of doing was yawn. So I did, not fooling Mama one bit. All of a sudden, I felt really sleepy, something I seemed to have passed to Sister and our guest. When Mama cut off the lamp again and she and Mother left the room, all three of us girls closed our eyes, said good night to each other and fell fast asleep. We slept until Saturday morning.

Morning came too soon. What had happened last night? I asked myself. Did someone come and steal it? I had no answers, only questions that needed answers.

I rubbed my eyes, burning from lack of enough sleep. I shook Sister and Delores. They both had bad breath and red eyes. I guessed mine were the same.

We all stretched and yawned before piling out of bed.

One by one, we used the bathroom, brushed our teeth, gargled, washed our faces, and left for the next girl to do the same. Then we went to the kitchen where Mama was making pancakes with syrup. She poured milk into three glasses.

I gulped my pancakes and milk down fast. So did Delores, though she tried to act ladylike. So did Sister. They both chewed fast and asked for seconds. Mama laughed, "Have you three been out plowing this morning?" We all laughed, and Delores offered, "You make the best pancakes, Mrs. Lowry, you really do."

Sister and I were shaking our head in agreement.

"She really does," Sister said.

"Yeah," I chimed in, "we get 'em most every Saturday. They melt in my mouth!"

"Oh, you girls are too much! What are you doing this morning?" she asked. "Just remember that we're going out to see your Aunt Babe and Uncle Jess in the county this afternoon! Babe's got some meat and vegetables for us. And some eggs."

"Oh, boy," I thought, "the country." There's nothing I liked best other than going out to the country.

"Is she gonna kill a chicken like she did last time?" I asked.

"Probably so, Doris, but I'm not quite sure. We'll just have to wait and see," she answered, walking out of the kitchen.

After we finished stuffing our faces and stomachs, we went in our room to dress. We chatted, as girls will do, about our friends, about what fashions we liked, about our favorites on TV, and of course, about boys—which ones were cute, which ones we liked, and which ones we couldn't stand.

We dressed in pedal pushers, knit shirts, bobby socks, and sneakers; combed our hair into upsweeps; and put bows and burettes in to hold down the flyaway parts.

We checked our money. Delores had two dollars; Sister and I had a dollar each. We were proud to have it since we didn't usually even have that amount all at one time.

We made the bed before we headed out to walk uptown to the Dime Store, where we'd spend. But on what?

We sang quietly as we walked, played "Don't Step on the Crack" as we walked. Like I said, we were heading for the Dime Store, McCrory's to be exact, straight to the candy counter. There was so much there, it was hard to make a choice. But I knew what I would get, and I told Delores, "The coconut squares are the best, girl!"

"No," Sister broke in, "get the blanched peanuts. They're all salty and everything and taste so good with a Coca-Cola."

"You don't even need a drink when you eat coconut squares." I put in.

"Yeah, but Doris, the coconut can get in your teeth. Yuck!"

Delores looked at us both standing at the counters trying to sell, like we were suddenly salesgirls for McCrory's. She chuckled and said, "I'm buying chocolate-covered peanuts. They're my absolute favorite!"

All Sister and I could do was laugh and peer at her. After all, she had the right to have her favorite, didn't she? Of course. Just like us.

We left McCrory's Five and Dime Store feeling quite grown up. We had to sneak pieces of what we'd bought into our mouths, for Mother had told us it wasn't polite to eat out on the street.

We looked in the stores at all the pretty things we didn't have the money to buy. We couldn't go in since there was no adult with us. That was the unwritten rule for colored children.

"I'd buy that," Delores laughed, pointing to a mother's dress in Belk's Department Store.

We walked on, laughing quietly, keeping our voices down like we'd been taught to do when we were out in public.

"Oh," Sister said, pointing at the next store, Raymond's. "I'm getting that!" She was pointing at this two-piece suit Mother or Mama would buy and wear to church. I thought it was horrible.

"Do you *really* like that, Sister?" I asked her. "Or are you just fooling us?"

"I'd really wear it, Doris. No fooling, scout's honor!"

"But you're not a scout, Sister."

"You don't have to tell me." That's all she said.

Remembering that we were going to the country, we started for home. I started the walking game Anna Lee had taught me, Skipping to the Barber Shop. "You start on your right foot, saying, 'Let's skip, let's skip, let's skip to the barber shop! Right now, let's skip, let's skip, let's skip to the barber shop...' And you keep chanting while skipping until someone gets out of step or steps on a line in the sidewalk." We giggled. Oh, what fun! Anna Lee would have loved this, but she was out of town with her family.

When we got home, happy and tired and full of candy and peanuts, Mama was waiting, standing in the kitchen, looking concerned.

"Girls, wash your hands and come get your lunch." It was bologna sandwiches, potato chips, and milk. "Make sure you clean those saucers. Nellie said we're leaving when you finish *and* make up your bed."

I wrinkled my nose—I hated that, often trading off with Sister for some other chore to do, like washing dishes. We gulped our lunch, still full of Dime Store favors. "Don't get that food on you," Mama ordered. "You're keeping these clothes on all day. You hear?" She looked at all of us, like she meant every word. She shot a quick, hot look at me. I had no comments.

We all nodded and answered, "Yes, m'am."

Meaning every word, we heard Mother's keys rattle. "Anybody who's got to use the bathroom, go now. There's no place to stop on the road."

At that, the three of us, all of a sudden, had to go—Delores, then Sister, me last.

"Girls," Mother inquired, "didn't you forget to do something this morning?"

We looked around at each other, knowing there was nothing we'd forgotten. Oh, oh, it dawned on Sister, spreading to the rest of us. The bed! We'd been so excited about walking uptown, we'd forgotten to make the bed! The three of us, long-faced, marched to our room. What a surprise—the bed was already made.

We looked from one to the other, then at the ladies who looked innocent. Finally, Mother spoke up, "I did it for you *this* time, but only *this* time. From now on, when you first get up, remember to make your bed. I'm your mama, not your maid." She was grinning, but I knew she'd meant every word.

"Okay, Mother, and thanks," Sister told her, hugging her wrist. "Yeah, Mrs. Ezell, thank you. We're sorry we forgot to make the bed." Mother patted her on the head. "Sorry, Mother," I put in my two cents. "It won't happen the next time," I offered.

Sister looked at me hard and blurted out, "Doris, there's not going to be a next time!"

"That's what I said!"

"Oh, hush, you two," Mother ended the interchange for us. "Let's all get in the car."

On the way out to Aunt Babe's, we looked at the horses running about in this huge, grassy field. There was a big sign which read: RIDE OUR HORSES. CHEAP PRICES. REDUCED PRICES FOR CHILDREN. SENIOR CITIZENS.

"Mother, can we come out here and ride this man's horses sometime?" I dared ask.

"We'll think about it, Doris, but that might be dangerous," she answered. "Horses can be like that, especially when they don't know you. You could get thrown off. Your neck could be broken!"

"Aw, Mother, that wouldn't happen," I protested.

"You might as well save your breath. You're *not*"—she emphasized that word—"going. And don't ask about it anymore. You'll be wasting breath!"

Delores patted my hand and glanced over at me about to cry. She tried to cheer me up by changing the subject. "Do you have any hobbies?" she asked, her voice sweet, girly, grown-up.

"No, not really. Do you?" I added, "I once sent away for a stamp kit. I was going to collect stamps."

"What happened?" she asked, interested. "Did it come, and did you start? My hobby is adding badges on my Girl Scout sash. I only have three: in cooking, sewing, and archery."

"That's neat." I stopped, looking at her; my eyes stretched, wide. "What's archery?" I asked her. I had heard the word, but in honesty, I had no clue as to what it meant.

Delores seemed happy to explain it. "Archery," she said, loud enough for everybody in the car to hear if they wanted to, "is using a bow and arrows to hit a bull's-eye." She went on to say, "It's like a sport or a game."

"It sounds like fun. I'm a Girl Scout too, troop 222. What troop are you in?" I inquired.

"My troop is number 329. We do lots of stuff like go fishing, go hiking and camping. One time, we stayed overnight in tents and slept in sleeping bags. The only bad thing about that was the rain that came in the middle of the night. "If it keeps raining," Ms. Falls, our troop leader, had awakened us and said, 'we'll have to pack up and leave.' We didn't want to leave, and the rain finally stopped. The next day, we made picnic beef soup in a big, black pot over a little stove. Boy, it was the best beef tomato soup I've ever eaten."

"*Wow*," I put in, "the only stuff my troop has ever done was put on a day camp one summer. We went from nine to five. We fished in a pond, cooked hot dogs over a fire, went on hikes, and did arts and crafts. We learned songs and played games. On the last day, we got awards and certificates. One time we went to the skating rink, and one Saturday we went to the movies and saw *The Trouble with Angels*. It was so funny!" We started laughing, giggling so hard about that movie until we got to Aunt Babe's house.

Mama looked at us as we got louder. "Now, girls, you must behave. Remember, your Uncle Sonny's not doing well."

"What's wrong with him?" I asked.

She looked back at me, saying, "Oh, he's just not doing well. He had the flu, and it's still in his system, Babe says," she explained. "Just remember what I said."

"Yes, m'am," I said. "We will."

Mother pulled the car near the entrance of the red dirt road, but before she could clear it, we heard children's deep voices screaming, "Yon dee come, here come our cousins! D from Roc' Hill: Doris 'N' Be-rah!"

"Mercy, mercy," was all I could say. We watched as they came all running barefoot up to the car and pressed their faces against the windows when Mother parked the car, looking in at us and grinning. One of them beckoned and said, "Y'all git out 'n com'on in de house." I think it was our cousin Dell, short for Dell a. They moved away only as Mother cut the car off, and we started getting out.

"Aunt Venie, Mama Lizzie say for y'all to com' on in de house. She ben feelin' kinda lo," Dell told us.

Mama asked, looking concerned, worried, "She's not in bed, is she?"

"N'om," was the answer. "She be in dere, but she up t'day. She in dere, waitin' for you."

We walked up the dusty porch to the brick but somewhat rickety house. Dell called through the screen door, "Ma Babe, dey here, dey here!" Aunt Babe was a short little woman who looked like Mama, except she had a crooked little smile from a stroke she'd had some years ago. We walked up on the porch, meeting her standing in the door. She was smiling and waving.

"Y'all come on in the house and have a seat." She waved us over to the green couch on the side. Her husband, my Uncle Jess, was sitting with his leg crossed. Uncle Sonny, with the one leg, sat on the cushiony armchair, pillows stacked neatly atop of each other. As always, he was humming while dipping snuff from a tin can. Every now and then, he'd spit a brown substance out in a tin cup.

When he finished, Uncle Sonny talked to his big sister Venie a little bit, then rolled a cigarette. He took a paper slip from a box with an Indian chief on it: Red Man was the product name. He, then, put some tobacco on the slip, rolled it out until it was long and narrow. Finally, he licked the inside flap and folded it over, sealing it up until it stayed in place.

He lit up, took a puff, and blew the smoke from his nose and mouth. He coughed a while, barely able to talk. When he could speak clearly, he warned, "Girls, don't *ever* bother with these things. Let your friends do it all they will, but don't you." He coughed. "These things'll kill you, beat up your lungs, and destroy your throats. You listen to me. I know what I'm talking about." He looked at Mother who was sitting in the wooden chair, looking down at her painted nails.

"Ain't that the truth, Nellie Mae?"

She looked at Uncle Sonny hard for a time. She shook her head in agreement. "You're certainly right about that, Uncle Sonny. These girls can't hear it any too soon. The temptation is all around, trying to get them to sin. No sir, they can't hear that any too soon or too much!"

"Venie, didn't you say you wanted a couple of chickens?" Aunt Babe asked Mama who was sitting comfortably, not wanting to stir. But to stir for free chickens, that was something else.

"Yeah, baby." She laughed, "That would help a lot. They've gotten so high, you can hardly buy them in the grocery store." Mama seemed gladder than glad at the chance for free anything.

Aunt Babe told Mama, "I've got butter, eggs, country ham, and sausage packed up for you. Now, we can go and get the chickens ready," Aunt Babe said. "You, chillin', can come too if you want. You might learn something new!" Delores, Sister, and I, wide-eyed and eager, shook our heads and let her know we wanted to see. Dell and our other cousins were still watching Delores. I hadn't introduced her, so I looked her way, saying, "Y'all, this is our friend, Delores Jeffers, up for the weekend. And Delores, these are our cousins Dell, Billy Boy, and Fat." They all looked from one to the other and back to the next and spoke. "Where you go to school?" Fat asked her.

"I go to Find Land Middle School. It's in Chess Hill. I'll be in seventh grade this coming next near," she told us. "Both Doris and I will be," she added.

"Come on, y'all," Aunt Babe ordered, walking toward the door.

We were all out in the yard among the clucking hens. I wondered if they knew what was coming. "Watch where you step, you chi'lums," Aunt Babe warned. She meant for where the chickens had used the bathroom on the ground.

She ran a chicken down and held it in both hands. All of a sudden, it was in her right hand, held by its neck, slinging it round and round until its body fell off. Blood squirted out of its neck onto its white body before falling to the ground. Then it flopped about on the ground, making a strange noise that sounded like a weak car horn. It flopped and flopped until it must have just gotten tired and stopped slowly, making that strange sound, like a weak car horn.

Aunt Babe picked up the hen by the feet and dropped it over in the brown croaker sack she had been holding, saying, "Now, Venie, you can take it over to the boiling water out in back in that big black pot to get the feathers off. I'll do the second hen meanwhile…" Her voice trailed off as Mama took the bag and headed toward the back of the house.

"I wonder what's going to happen now," Delores said, her eyes round and big.

"You see's, jess you wait," Dell told her. We trotted out behind Mama, wanting to see what was coming next. We could already see steam rising out of this big black pot sitting on a pile of large smoking sticks.

Mama reached into the blood-drenched bag and pulled out the headless hen by its leg. She lowered it carefully, slowly, down into the boiling, bubbling water. She brought it back up really fast, but almost hesitating, like she'd forgotten what came next.

Holding the fowl by one leg, she began to pluck the feathers off, one by one at first, then by the fistfuls. She continued until we were looking at a grocery store found chicken, the kind you saw in Winn-Dixie.

"You wanna hold it?" she asked us, laughing. We all jumped back, that is, all except our cousins, who were used to seeing chickens get killed and prepared for eating.

Mama repeated the steps on the second misfortunate hen still strutting around, unknowing what its destiny held.

"Would you chi-lums like some milk? It's got cream on it," Aunt Babe had urged earlier. Sister and I knew what that meant. We'd had the sweet cream before, and we remembered how good it had tasted. Aunt Babe had finished up and came where we were. "It's good," I told Delores and saw Sister's head nodding in agreement. Aunt Babe gave the next dead chicken to Mama.

"Let me wash my hands," she told us, going over to the pump. She led us into the kitchen and poured three glasses midway. "See how you like this." She smiled—her crooked one.

The cream eased down my throat, prompting me to say, "Um, this is good. May I *please* have some more, Aunt Babe? Pretty, please!" She bent over, laughing from her gut. "If there was more, but that's it!"

Dell was looking hard. "I didn't ev'n not git non," she said, looking really hard at Aunt Babe.

Mama came around where we were, holding both the plucked chickens. "Babe," she pondered, "how're the plums doing? Have you picked any yet?"

"We picked a few," she paused, put her hands on her hips, "when dat fros' come de other week, it took an kill all o'dem pretty much. We kin go see if 'n dey out dere nah!"

The women started to a rocky, dusty path near the back of the yard. It led into a wooded area, where a green vine was growing. We saw a few red little somethings. *There must be the plums there*, I thought.

She picked one and gave it to me. "Taste one, you child," Aunt Babe said, looking at me. I obeyed, popping the fruit open inside my mouth, tasting its sweetness. I could get used to this, I thought. There were many plums on the vines, and when we left, there hung not a one. Delores had plucked—and eaten her first plum.

We all walked back to the house. Uncle Jess teased, "Y'all better be careful! That ole man's still out dere. He go git you. Don' go back out dere!"

"What old man?" Delores, Dell, and I were shaking, trembling, scared. He might really know about some old man.

Mother smiled and looked over at Mama who was standing near the door with a couple of bags in her hands. "Well, all," she said, looking around at all of us from where we stood or sat. "I guess we should be going. It was so good to see all of you. You look so well."

"Thank you, Nellie, honey. We doin' pretty good, *'about like trees walkin'.*" We all chuckled.

Uncle Jess hugged us all; all except my cousins. He was used to them. He opened the screen door, holding it open, though insects were buzzing in. Aunt Babe was smiling her crooked smile. She hugged us and told us be good and to come back soon. She and Mama, arm in arm, strolled out in front of us and stood by the car.

"Venie, all of y'all looks real good," Aunt Babe said. They hugged.

"Thank you, baby."

"Com' bac' real soon to see us's."

Mother unlocked the doors, opened them, and watched while we got it. She opened the trunk so Mama could load what we'd been given. We were off, making our way back the same way we'd come.

Delores offered before being asked. "Wow, I had the best time ever! I never thought fried chicken came that way, jumping all over the ground, getting blood everywhere, and having no head anymore! And what about the plums?"

I egged her on. "They were the best, the sweetest, weren't they? Oh, yummy. And we really picked them!"

"We sure did!" She agreed, laughing down deep in her throat. Aunt Babe had packed some plums for us to take home.

We had waved and hugged and waved and hugged for the longest time before getting in the car, something I'll always remember—those good old country ways. Delores, I knew, would remember those good times, too.

Riding home, Sister, Delores, and I all went to sleep. I opened my eyes and rubbed them, just as Mother was turning into the driveway.

"Wake up, girls. We're home!" she sang.

Delores yawned and stretched. She looked over at Sister and said, "Wake up, Sister Vera, we're home!" We all three giggled and got ready to go into the house, tired, but happy.

"Mrs. Lowry and Mrs. Ezell, I had so much fun out there! I thank you for taking me," Delores said, standing in the kitchen.

"Well, isn't that nice?" Mother said. "Did you get to see the chickens get killed? That was something else, wasn't it?"

"Oh, yes," Delores laughed. "I'd never seen anything like that before. I'll think of it from now on every time I eat chicken."

Mama told her, "Well, honey, tomorrow you'll be thinking about it. We always have chicken on Sunday!"

"Yes, m'am."

"What do you want to do now?" I asked.

"I know, let's play cards," Delores suggested, heading to our room. "I brought some with me." She started going through her suitcase. "At least, I thought I brought some." She didn't have them. "Sorry, y'all," she put her head down, moping.

"Oh, that's okay, girl," Sister pitched in. "You can't remember everything."

"I know." I put in. "We could play with my paper dolls! I'll get' em out." I offered.

"Doris, we can't. You lost the little round things they stand in. Remember?" Sister reminded me.

"Oh, that's right, Delores. Just last week."

"Well, what if we go outside and play?" she suggested.

"Yeah," Sister shouted, sounding eager. "We're going out, y'all," she called to Mother and Mama who were in the kitchen.

We kept walking around the block, trying to stay on the same 'stop'. We giggled and skipped and chanted a little song. We waved to Mrs. Dickers who was sitting on her porch. A man went by, walking his dog on a leash. He growled.

"Do you have a dog, Delores?" I asked her, twirling around.

"Not anymore. I had one once, but he got killed."

"How?" I asked, feeling sorry for her.

"He was chasing a car, and the car hit him. He died right there on the spot. Mommy said next year, she's getting me another one—a poodle," she told us.

Delores, Vera, and Doris in
Their Easter Clothes

"Oh, poodles are so cute." I beamed. "I wish we had a dog, but Mama says they're too hard to take care of. Plus she said she'd end up taking care of it."

We circled the block a few more times before going in. It was just too pretty a day to be in the house, though it did seem to be getting late. When we walked around one more time, Sister said, sounding like a grown-up, "Let's go on in now, y'all. I'm tired."

Delores and I didn't say anything. We just went in the house right behind her. "You girls, wash your hands. We're going to eat," Mama called. "I've soon got to leave."

We gathered at the kitchen table to a meal of cubed steak, mashed potatoes, and string beans. We ate, talking little, for Mother and Mama were talking about somebody's husband leaving in the family car with some other woman. I wanted to ask who the people were, but I certainly knew what would have happened if I'd dare. The food was really good, and all three of us girls got seconds.

The three of us cleared the table, got the dishes washed, dried, and put away. We washed the table down, swept, and even mopped the floor.

"Well," Mother beamed, coming into the kitchen, "what's gotten into the three of you? And how much are you charging?" She was smiling broadly.

"Aw, Mother," I chimed, "we just gave you the Easter night special."

"Easter's not until tomorrow, Doris," Sister announced like it was big news.

"All right, you two," Mother cautioned, looking straight at me.

"Dinner was so good!" I said again, making sure everybody knew.

We girls were watching *Gunsmoke* when a big blue-and-white Buick pulled up to the front door. The car horn blew.

Mama had kissed us already and warned us to be good. We promised that we would. She strutted down the sidewalk, wearing her blue-and-white checkered cotton dress. She carried a starched white apron and a pink sweater in case it cooled off.

We watched the white man lean over and open the back car door. A big old golden looking dog jumped up against the window on the passenger's side. The man let the dog get in to the back, brushed the front seat off, and helped Mama into the car. The dog's paws were against the back window pane as the car pulled off.

"That was Mr. Hardsen. He has three children, two boys and a girl," I told Delores. "They're nice. They've given us their old toys, and Nancy sent me a few dresses she outgrew," I added. "But I didn't really like them."

"Yeah," Sister told her, "but Mama made you wear them anyway."

"Only to school a couple of times." I clarified.

As the night wore on, we watched cowboys until it was time for baths. Mother started the water while we got out our pajamas and hairnets. "Now remember, girls, no fooling around. Get your baths and straight to bed! You hear me, don't you?" she ordered, sounding really strict.

"Yes, Mother!" Sister and I piped together. "Yes, Mrs. Ezell," Delores laughed.

As the three of us were going into the bathroom, we heard the side doorbell chime twice. Sister said, getting into the tub, "That got to be Attorney Bennett, Mother's 'special friend'."

"I know about those 'special friends'." Delores laughed. "Mommy's got one too."

"Remember last night, y'all," I asked, "when we played around with the bubbles?" We all laughed, remembering quite well.

It was Attorney Bennett, I knew by Mother's laugh. He was a very nice handsome man who had known Mother and Daddy since their college days. Delores laughed and said, "Our Mamas are something else, aren't they, y'all?" Sister and I shook our head up and down.

We finished our baths with little playing this time. We brushed our teeth after putting on our pajamas. Delores and I thought we should sleep in our own instead of trading as we'd planned. We didn't want to get in trouble. We brushed our teeth and put our hairnets on.

"Good night, Mother and Attorney Benett," Sister and I called. Delores echoed, "Goodnight, Mrs. Ezell and Attorney Benett."

"Oh, come here, girls, and speak." She directed us, and we trotted into the living room where they were sitting on the couch.

"Hi, Attorney Bennett," we plugged. "How've you been?" I asked, smiling.

Before he could respond, Mother pulled Delores forward. "Harry, this little lady is Delores. She's our house guest up for Easter weekend".

He stood, smiled down at her, and shook her hand. "Well, well, another pretty young lady. I thought Vera and Doris were the only two in town." We all smiled. "Hello, Attorney Bennett, it's nice to meet you." "Are you having a good time up here?" he asked.

"Oh, yes, sir, I'm having so much fun. Doris and Sister Vera are just like my own sisters. See, I just have brothers," she told him.

"How many?" he asked. "Three, one older and two younger brothers. They're David, Donald, and Dennis. They're with my daddy this weekend."

He breathed hard and said, "I see."

"Well, girls, would you like some ice cream before you go to bed?"

We squealed, scared to believe our good fortune. It was no special occasion, just time for ice cream! "Oh, yes, m'am!" we all exclaimed. Sister and I had never gotten it at night, except one other time last winter when I had had my tonsils taken out.

"Hurry and eat, now. You've got to get in bed. Church tomorrow, remember?"

"Yes, m'am." We nodded, fixing our bowls.

She looked at Attorney Bennett. "Would you like some?"

"Don't mind if I do," he answered, eyeing our ice cream. "I just love chocolate."

Mother filled his bowl to the brim. She reached it to him, smiling. Then she reminded us to hurry with ours.

After we had slurped and licked until nothing was left, we put our bowls in the sink, hugged Mother who kissed our cheeks and foreheads, then said, "Off to bed, and go right to sleep right away. I mean it." We nodded and told Attorney Bennett good night. As soon as we were snug in the bed, we went straight to sleep, with no night games and playing around.

The night was easy, and so was our breathing. We slept peacefully. I saw dreams as pastel, as pink, yellow, blue, green, and gold as the bright colors in the rainbow. The dream floated through my head easily, so much so that the night had all of a sudden became a clear, sunny morning.

I rubbed my eyes, thinking about my new Easter dress, shoes, and pocketbook. And white anklet socks with lace trim and black patent leather shoes. Sister had the same. We would have on our wide-tail crinoline slips, white and fluffy.

I sat up, up in bed, shook Sister and Delores who still slept. "Wake up, wake up," I trickled. Slowly, slowly, they stretched and yawned. "Hi, y'all," I giggled. We scrambled out of the bed and hurried to brush our teeth and wash our faces. Then we went out to the kitchen where Mama and Mother were. They hugged and kissed the three of us. "Good morning, girls, and happy Easter," Mother offered. "How did you sleep?"

"I had a good dream," I said, all smiles. "Me, too," declared Sister. "So did I," Delores followed.

"Well!" Mother quirked. Mama just stood there, looking, trying not to laugh.

We always had fried chicken and gravy on Sunday mornings. Not this morning, for on the table was a stack of golden pancakes beside a plate of sausage patties. Glasses of milk were there also. Sitting at the breakfast table, we waited to get our food, trying hard to be patient. I just couldn't wait, so I pinched off a bit of sausage and started it toward my mouth. Mama saw what was happening and slapped it out of my hand. "We haven't said the grace yet, Doris. You know better! Now let's bow our heads." She purred.

We did, and Mama prayed. After grace, she put two pancakes on each plate, followed by a circle of country sausage. Everything smelled so good, too. "Before you get dressed," Mama told us, "let's take a look in the dining room." We finished eating quickly, anxious to see what she meant. She led us over to the table where there sat three Easter baskets. "The children sent them. You'll have to thank them," she told us. The baskets were so pretty, all filled with colored eggs and candy, all among artificial green grass blades. In the very center sat a chocolate bunny, munching an orange carrot.

"Mama, how did they know to send three?" Sister asked her.

"I mentioned we had a little visitor for the weekend, our little Delores. Mary sent you her basket, Delores, so you would have one, too."

Delores was all smiles. "That was so nice of her. May I call her now and thank her?" she pondered.

"I don't think so, dear. They're getting ready for church. But you can write out a thank-you note after church before we eat dinner."

She ushered us out of the dining room and back into the kitchen. "Okay, girls, let's clear the table and get the dishes washed, quickly, so you can dress for church."

"When can we open our baskets, Mama?" I asked.

"After church," she answered. "Now let's get a move on. Wash your hands and faces, put on deodorant and powder and Vaseline. Then put on your clothes and shoes and socks."

"Yes, m'am," we said, our voices as one. The three of us went into our room to find the bed made and clothes laid out.

Mother was waiting for us. "Girls, when you're dressed, come let me see what I can do to those heads."

"Oh, Mother," Sister said, "I can do my own hair. Thanks, anyway."

"Come on, Doris, you first," Mother said, holding out the comb, brush, and Vaseline.

"You're not gonna put grease in my hair?" I groaned.

"Aw, Doris, just around the edges. And a little between the parts," she laughed, knowing how much I hated having Vaseline in my hair. Mother eased into the straight chair while I slid between her legs. Instantly, I started flinching, knowing what was coming. "Hold still, Doris, I don't have time for this foolishness!"

"Yes, Mother, but you *know* just how tender-headed I am."

Mother squeezed her legs around me until I could feel the pressure build. I twitched. "Hold still, Doris," Mother warned. She yanked, and she brushed and combed, doing the actions until she'd worked the Vaseline into my locks. She did it again until the hair seemed tamed enough to be fixed for church.

She handed me the mirror with the handle on it. "See how you like it." She beamed.

I looked at my hair, satisfied, but not wanting to admit it. "Yes, m'am," is all I had to say.

"Delores, you're next!" Mother said, taking her gently by the arm. When she was placed, Mother put the towel around her shoulders, same as she'd done with me. "Are you tender-headed like my two?" Mother asked.

"A little bit, Mrs. Ezell, especially when I get my hair washed, and it has to be combed out. That's when I cry my eyes out," she answered.

Mother went through the same motions with Delores as she had with me, combing and brushing until she had all the naps and kinks out. When she had finished, Delores had a nice, bouncy pony-tail hanging from a green rubber band, just like mine.

"Vera," Mother called. "Come on in and let me check your hair." Sister had been in the bathroom fixing her hair. When she came in, Mother patted it down and pulled a few loose strands in place. "Nice," she said, adding, "you three, get your pocketbooks and sit on the couch. We'll be ready in a few minutes. Get some tissue, too. Can't let you have nasty noses!"

We sat on the couch and spoke quietly. While waiting, we looked in each other's pocketbooks. I took Delores's while she took mine. Then she looked in Sister's, and Sister looked in hers. Next, Sister looked in mine, and I looked in Sister's. We had the same stuff, except Delores had a dollar and three quarters. Plus fifteen cents. She had spent a dime on candy yesterday. Sister and I didn't get our Sunday money yet. We watched Mother and Mama come out down the hall, all dressed up in their Easter clothes. I thought they looked like queens.

"Mrs. Lowry and Mrs. Ezell," Delores said to them, "you both look so very pretty."

Sister and I both agreed. "Yep, you sure do," I told them.

"You're really pretty," Sister said.

They thanked us, and Mother told us to go out to the car. Mother locked the house up, and we five trailed out to the car into the beautiful April morning.

As we got into the car, I said, "Y'all, Delores has got a whole lot of money!"

"That's none of your business, Doris," Mama chimed in. "Besides, how do you know how much money she had? You just be thankful for what you have!"

"Yes, m'am," I answered.

When we got to church, Mother gave Sister and me money for Sunday school and church. We got a dime each for Sunday school and fifteen cents for church. Boy, the stuff I could have bought at the little red store. But no, I had to pay it in church. Old Satan was sure tempting me.

When we got to church, people were pulling in. Mother parked in her usual spot. We all got out and walked toward the church. As we climbed the steps, our shoes clicked, clicked, clicked on the pavement and brick steps.

Sister, Delores, and I went to the same class—the Intermediates. Mrs. Maddison was our teacher. She had a high-pitched voice, and she loved to talk. She was young, married, and had three children. She was staring hard at Delores, so I spoke up, "Mrs. Maddison, this is our friend, Delores Jeffers. She is visiting us for the weekend, and she lives in Chess Hill, and she's in the sixth grade, just like me." I was going to say more, but Mrs. Maddison was looking like she wanted to zip up my lips.

She started smiling, and she said, hugging Delores, "Why, hello, dear. We're glad you're here this gorgeous morning. Class, this is our new friend, Delores Jeffers, from Chess Hill. Make her feel welcome, you hear. Oh, she's Doris and Vera's friend."

"Hi, Delores," everybody chimed in.

Delores smiled and nodded. She seemed happy to be here with all of us. Mrs. Maddison explained why we celebrated Easter every year, about the death and resurrection of our Savior, how we would have to accept Him and ask Him to forgive our sins and receive the Holy Spirit if we wanted to go to heaven when we died. *Wow!* So that was it—the whole reason we were to believe in Jesus and God. Why hadn't they (the preachers) all just said it? It was so easy. I'd ask Mama about it. She would know.

Mrs. Maddison stopped talking and had us all to make a double line, girls in front. There were more girls than boys, so she put a few boys in our line to even it out. "All of you look so nice, I wanted to get a picture. Now smile really pretty for me. Say C-H-E-E-S-E! All together, now, one, two, three." She held up her camera and adjusted the lens. Then flash went the bulb. I think my eyes closed. She then gave us a piece of candy as she passed the collection plate. Coins clanged as the children dropped their money in. When all was finished, she looked at a girl.

"Becky, will you count the money please, and fill out the white slip, and take it when we go up?" she asked, handing over the brown plate. Becky shook her head yes and smiled, taking the plate.

"Let's line up and go quietly up. All the classes may not be through. And class, Happy Easter. I'll see you this afternoon at the Easter egg hunt." She opened the door. "Let's go up. And Delores, you come back soon to see us, you hear? We really enjoyed having you here with us. So you come back."

"Yes, m'am. I'll try," Delores answered with a smile. We walked quietly up the steps into the half-empty church. We sat in two rows near the front. "I like your Sunday school teacher," Delores whispered to me.

"Yeah, she's really nice," I agreed, keeping my voice down. "Smart, too. She knows her *Bible*," I added.

Mrs. Maddison looked down our aisle and hushed us up. Soft music started playing as classes entered the sanctuary. Girls were dressed up all in frills and lace and bonnets on their heads. The boys wore their blue suits, starched white shirts and neckties or bow ties. The ladies had on new dresses and hats high heel shoes.

We all knew this was a special time. Easter, next to Christmas, was the best time of year. We children watched as the other classes came in. We were joyfully singing songs of the season as they came in.

Soon, Rev. Rudder came in and went to his pulpit. Church was about to start. The children went to different areas to sit, some with their parents, some toward the back where they could whisper, draw pictures on the programs, and chew bubble gum. (I had once tried sitting in the back; Mama had spotted me and had come back, gotten me by the arm, and marched me back to the front. How embarrassed I had been as I'd heard the giggles coming from the children.)

Rev. Rudder looked like a king in his white robe, trimmed in gold with a gold-and-green sash around his neck and shoulders. Sister, Delores, and I were sitting on the bench across from Mama and Mother. I hated it because I couldn't even whisper or giggle, not even when Miss Barber would stand up, wave her arms, and cry, "Ho-lee! Ho-lee! Ho-lee!" She'd keep doing it until an usher would hurry over and pat her, settling her down. I'd want to laugh, but I knew better.

Delores wrote a note on her program and passed it over to me along with the pencil. I read it, answered, and was getting ready to pass it when I saw Mama looking at us. "Oh, no," I thought, easing the program into the pages of the songbook lying in my lap.

Rev. Rudder's sermon came to an end, but if I'd had to write a summary of it, I'd have made a D+. My mind had been on the egg hunt that would take place later on. We sang an Easter song, followed by the closing hymn. Rev. Rudder said the closing prayer and dismissed his congregation to the dinner being served downstairs.

Mother beckoned us over to them, and we started out to the car. "Are we staying for dinner here?" Sister asked her. "We have dinner at home," she said. We got in the car and were home in no time.

"How did you like the services and Sunday school, Delores?" Mother asked as we were walking into the house.

"They were fine, Mrs. Ezell, all of them were," she answered. "I really liked the Sunday school teacher. She was really nice."

"Yes, Mrs. Maddison is a very good woman. We've known her for a long time, her whole family."

"Yes, m'am."

"May we wear our Easter dresses to the egg hunt, Mama?" I inquired, just loving my dress more and more.

"My goodness, no, Doris. You'd get them dirty!" Mama barked in alarm. "Let me take your picture while you're still dressed," Mother told us as we walked toward the house. "I'll go in and get the camera."

"Okay," Sister said, finding where we'd stand. Mother went into the house, soon coming back with the camera. It was Sister's Brownie Starflash that she'd gotten for Christmas. Santa had left it among other things. Daddy had come through this time, making all of us happy.

"All right, girls, let's get ready for the picture," Mother sang as she came out where we were. "Stand over there, out of the glare." She directed. Mother wasn't that good at taking pictures, but she had gotten better. We did, letting Sister get in the middle. "Now, smile real pretty, girls." Mother directed, "One, two, three! Got it! Now let me get one of each of you. Vera, you go first, then Delores, last Doris."

"Why can't I be first?" I laughed.

"Would you like to be neither?" Mother asked me, and she was not smiling. "Delores, when we get the pictures back, I'll mail some to y'all. How's that?" Mother promised.

"Oh, thank you, Mrs. Ezell, I don't take good pictures. I always shut my eyes," she said.

"These are going to be good ones, I just bet." Mother encouraged. "You girls are mighty pretty in your fancy dresses."

I looked around at us; we were all smiles. Taking pictures was fun, posing in all different ways until you get just the right one. "Mother," I asked as we were going in, "may we wear our dresses to the Easter egg hunt?"

"Goodness, no, Doris. You'd get them all dirty. You'll wear your pedal pushers. Now let's go in and eat. I'm hungry!" Well, that was that!

When we were changed into our play clothes, our fancy dresses hanging up again, and Delores's packed away in her suitcase, we gathered in the dining room for Easter dinner. It was different. There was a whole ham with circles of pineapple all around it, potato salad, green beans, sweet potatoes, rolls, and coconut cake for dessert. If I'd had my way, we'd have started with the cake.

"Let's everybody get seated," Mama told us. When we did, she stood, bowed her head, and said, "Let us pray." Her prayer over dinner was a sweet one, a minisermon even, that took in all the points of living and of Easter. It made me sorry for all the bad things I had done: hit Sister for no reason, talked about a girl at school behind her back, and giggled when Tommy Barlett had blurted out a wrong answer in arithmetic.

I was thinking, *Mama, please hurry up*, just as she was saying, "*Amen.*" As soon as grace was over, the clatter of eating utensils meeting platters, mouths, dishes, bowls and plates, along with quiet conversation, filled the room.

Mother and Mama alike put food items on our plates. They poured sweet tea into our fancy Sunday glasses. The ice tingled.

(Mother had held the glass while Mama poured.) Boy, did the food taste good! "Delores, what's your favorite food?" I asked, putting more sweet potatoes into my mouth.

"Oh, I don't really know," she answered quietly. We'd all been taught when eating at the table, especially on the Lord's day, to keep our voices down. "I guess I like French fried potatoes and hamburgers. And I love coconut cake!" she laughed, looking at the cake Mama had baked.

"My favorite's hot dogs," I chimed.

"And I love blanched peanuts," Sister told us.

"Mrs. Ezell and Mrs. Lowry, this food surely is good," Delores told them, dabbing at the corners of her mouth with the napkin. She straightened it back out and put it in her lap.

"Always use good table manners," they'd always taught us. And we did. "Anyone want seconds?" Mama coaxed.

"I'm getting a bit more potato salad," Mother told us.

"It's so delicious."

"Sure is," Sister agreed, rubbing her stomach.

"Eat up, now, girls. We have plenty, remember," Mother told us.

"I'm ready for cake!" I volunteered.

Mother looked over at my plate, still with food on it. "You don't get dessert," she said, "until that plate is clean. Remember?"

"Yes, Mother," I told her, starting to eat again. I wanted cake and wanted it now!

"Doris, don't eat so fast. You'll choke yourself," Mother chided, "and wipe that mouth! Mind your manners, hear."

"Yes, m'am," I answered, wiping my mouth. I remembered to put the napkin back in my lap. In less than three more gulps, I was finished. Cake time.

Mother shot an eye at me, and said, "Doris Amurr, you're *too* much. Let Mama cut you off some cake."

Mama, finally, took the cake knife up, walked over, and stood over the cake. "I hope I got it right. I didn't bake it 'till I came home last night from babysitting. Didn't they send you three girls some nice baskets? And they didn't have to do that. Just the kindness of their hearts, that all it was."

"Yes, it was, Mama," Sister told her.

Delores and I were nodding our heads yes. "Let them know we thank them a lot, please, Mama," I pitched in.

"No, you've got to thank them. After all, they sent the baskets to *you*," she stressed.

"I'd like to send a note," Delores said.

"Mommy always makes me send a note when somebody gives me something." "That's fine, honey," Mama told her. "All three of you can send them thank-you notes." We've got homework when there's not even any school going on, I thought, daring not to say it.

The egg hunt was scheduled from two to four. Mother dropped us off at two sharp. Three grown-ups and several other children were already there, including two known bullies, Tom Ellis and Mark Jones, who went to my school. They were always in trouble and lived in the principal's office. I had heard that they were smart and could have made good grades if they had only tried.

When other children had come along with several other grown-ups, Rev. Rudder gave the rules, blew the starting whistle, and counted one, two, three, go! We started, looking everywhere—in the grass along the church, in the shrubs, in the flowerpots. I found a purple egg in the grass and plopped into my plastic bag. I spread open a bush and found a second egg, this one blue. I was about to stick my hand into the flowerpot that was swinging when I heard, "I saw it first." I think it was Mark. "You know I did!"

"It's mine," Tom called back. And before you knew it, the two boys were scrambling around on the ground, getting their clothes all messed up. We children were no longer kneeling, looking for colored eggs, but standing up to see what was going on. A couple of the grown-ups were already on the scene and had each boy by the arm or collar.

I saw Mrs. Armstrong wagging her finger at Tom, her mouth going. I couldn't hear what she was telling him, but I could imagine the lines: "You know better! You know you do" or something like that. Mr. Neal, who taught the juniors, was blasting Mark the same way. Imagination is wonderful, for mine knew exactly what had been said in the end: "Either get it together or leave!"

The scuffle had put a damper on the hunt. Our voices weren't as joyous; our faces hung down. Yet when the hunt was over, I had five eggs in my bag, Sister had four, and Delores had a whopping six. Rev. Rudder blew the whistle. Carol Sims, one of the older girls, won a silver dollar for finding ten eggs—the most. Tim Adams had found the golden egg. He got a chocolate bunny.

Our eggs were divided equally and fairly among us. We each got three eggs to take home, even the winners. Three measly colored Easter eggs, and I probably wouldn't even eat them, cold boiled eggs with rainbow-colored shells on them. Oh, well, what could be better?

"How was the hunt?" Mother asked as she drove us home.

"Good," Delores blurted out, quick to answer. "There was almost a fight between these two boys, but the grown-ups broke it up."

"Do tell," Mother responded. "Who were the boys? Doris, Vera, did you know them?"

"I know them," Sister answered. "They don't go to our church, just live near it. Tom and Mark are their first names."

"I declare," Mother seemed livid, "fighting at the Lord's house! No home training, that's what. Those boys just need a good switch."

"What they need is love" I wanted to tell her. I had heard how one's mother ran the streets at night; how the other's father beat him mercilessly. Rumor? Does the truth really win in the end? Sometimes, Mother and Mama could make me get real mad, but to tell the truth, I knew they really loved me, and Sister, too.

When we got home, a snack was waiting: vanilla ice cream and coconut cake. This was the best Easter I could ever remember, and I told them so, wiping crumbs from around my mouth with the back of my hand.

"Doris, where are your table manners?" Mama chided." What do you think your napkin's for?"

"I don't have one!"

"And whose fault is that? You know you don't sit at the table without a napkin."

"Yes m'am," I answered sheepishly, going to the kitchen for a napkin. I saw Sister trying to hold her laughter in. She coughed a couple of times, like any minute she'd explode.

Delores just said, "Mrs. Lowry, this cake is mighty good. And you say you baked it last night when you got home? But weren't you tired?" She sounded really concerned.

"Oh, honey, when you get to be my age, you stay sleepy and tired."

"My mother says the same thing. I guess it's about being you and mommy's age."

"Yes, honey. Would you like more cake? You're welcome, you know."

"Yes, m'am, I know. But no thank you. I couldn't hold another bite, as good as it is."

"All right then. I guess Vera and Doris are feeling about the same." Maybe Vera, but certainly not Doris, I thought, ready for a third piece of cake. It was just a thought; that's all it ever was.

We helped clear the table after our snacks were over and offered to wash the dishes and put them away. "Who invented cake?" I asked out of the blue. Everybody stopped. Life in slow motion, like something you would see on *The Twilight Zone*. I saw Mother look at Mama, and Mama look at Mother. They went back and forth and back and forth. Finally, Mother, half-laughing, half-frowning, asked the question, "Doris, where *do* you get all those silly notions from?"

I thought, but dared not say, "What silly notions?" For I saw nothing silly about my question. "M'am?" It's all I said, all I could say.

Grown-ups could be something else. They thought the same about us children and oftentimes said it, "Why don't you three walk around and see Mrs. Benson?" Mrs. Benson was an old lady who lived a few streets over. She had seven children, but they all lived somewhere else. She once had told Mama she was moving out to live with her son in Denver, but she never did. She had a finger that would not bend on her right hand, and she knew everything about the *Bible*. She and Mama talked on the telephone every day, sometimes more.

Following that suggestion, we walked the streets over to Mrs. Benson's. Hers was a plank house that badly needed painting, but the inside was neat and clean and full of her treasures. We hopped up the steps, knocked, and waited. "Who knock?" she called.

"It's us, Doris, Vera and Delores!" Sister called in a soft-loud voice. We saw the blinds part, heard keys rattle, and the door squeaked open.

"Oh, it's you, girls, Doris and Vera. Well, well, well. How nice to see you. Yes, yes. My, my. Come on in the house, you girls. How's Mama?" she stopped talking and took a hard look at Delores. "And who's this girl?"

"Oh, Mrs. Benson, this is our friend, Delores Jeffers, up to the weekend," Sister offered. "She lives in Chess Hill."

"And she's in the same grade as me!" I added, like that was important for her to know.

"Well, well, hello, Miss Delores," Mrs. Benson said, all businesslike. "It's mighty nice to have you in our little town. Are you having a good time?"

"Oh, yes, m'am," Delores responded. "I'm having a great time! We've been doing so much."

"That's nice, honey," Mrs. Benson cut in. "Would you girls like some cake and lemonade?"

Still full from dinner dessert, we declined the offer. "No, thank you, Mrs. Benson," Sister offered. Delores and I nodded and smiled. "How are your children doing?" I spoke up to change the subject.

"They doing real good. They all up north now. I don't get to see them that much anymore. But they call me every week and send me money, too. Every month, those envelopes come in. Yeah, I got good children. They don't forget they old mama." She stopped talking, and her eyes got sad. She shook her head, like she had a secret about each one of her children. "Would you like to see their pictures?" she asked.

"Yes, m'am," we all said in one voice.

She led us to a room in the rear of her home. Neatly displayed on the wall were seven framed smiling faces, girls and boys. She started at one side of the wall, pointing upward toward a picture. "Now, this is Carl Lee Jr., named for his daddy. He look just like his daddy, too."

We nodded and smiled. "He's handsome," Sister snickered.

"Oh, yes," Mrs. Benson beamed, pointing to the next picture. "Now this is my daughter, Mae Helen. She's in nursing school. This is my next son, Jacky. He's in the army. And this is little Toney Ann. She's a teacher." Mrs. Benson looked at us, pride in her eyes. "Their father, rest his soul, and me, by the grace of God, spent many a sleepless night trying to figure out how we'd get them all through school. But thank the good Master, we did. Carl's looking down from heaven right this minute!" She moved on farther, pointing to the next picture. "And this lad is Henry. He's a policeman out in Oregon. Yeah, way out in Oregon. Why he had to go way out there, I just don't know. But that's where he is. Out in Oregon." She moved on and pointed. "Now this is my son, Sammy Lee. Sammy Lee is a chef. He always did like fiddling around in the kitchen when I'd be in it. He loved to try to help me with the cooking. How his brothers and sisters would laugh. But he didn't seem to mind." She glowed with a mother's pride. Her smile grew even wider as she pointed to the last picture on the wall. "And girls," she paused and breathed heavily. "This is George, my big baby," she laughed heartedly. "He's out in Arizona, working on a ranch, branding horses. When he's not doing that, he works as a policeman." She smiled widely.

"Well, Mrs. Benson," Sister told her, "you surely do have some nice-looking children, pretty daughters and handsome sons."

"Yes, m'am, you do," I chimed in.

Delores agreed, "You really do."

"Well, thank you, girls. That's mighty sweet of y'all to say. Mighty sweet. Uh-huh, mighty sweet."

"I guess we should be going, Mrs. Benson," Sister said, heading toward the door.

"Carl Lee Jr. say he go get the house painted next spring," she offered. "I'll be *so* glad. It need it real bad, right now, and I just can't afford to get it painted myself with just my little check coming in each month and what my children sends. It's sho' been nice having y'all visit me, girls, Doris, Vernie and De-lois. Y'all come back anytime, just anytime. All three of you, well, you so pretty, so pretty." She was grinning from one end to the other.

"Good-bye, Mrs. Benson, and Happy Easter!" we called together.

"Good-bye, girls. Tell Mama I'll talk with her soon."

"That's a nice lady," Delores said as we trudged up the street home.

"Yes, she is," Sister said. "We've know her a long time. She's one of Mama's best friends, too."

"I had a good time at her house," Delores told us. "I like her wall of children."

"Me too," I said.

We were quiet the rest of the way home, each lost in thought. I was thinking about Mrs. Benson's seven children, all working except the one in nursing school. And soon, she'd be working, too.

Finally, we were home. We went bolting into the house that seemed to be waiting for us to come home. "How was everything at Mrs. Benson's?" Mama asked, coming in where we were.

"Just fine, Mama," I answered. "We had the best time. She showed us pictures of all seven of her children. Can you believe anybody with seven children? Seven? Four, maybe, but seven?" I puffed, out of breath.

"Well, Doris," Mama spoke up. "People had big families back then. The children would help out in the fields and on the farms. You don't see that happening much now these days."

"Oh," I said, "that's why there are only two children in our family?" I dared asked, hoping not to get hit.

When I didn't, I dared to even ask another question, "Mama?"

"Yes, baby?" Mama probed. "Where is Mr. Benson?"

Mama gave me a sharp look that translated *trouble* to me. She looked from girl to girl, each one waiting, and wanting, the answer as bad as the other. I looked around. "Where's Mother?" I asked.

"Mr. Benson died a few years ago from some strange virus," Mama answered. "And your mama went to Lucy Sampson's for a while," Mama told us. Mrs. Sampson, also a teacher like Mother, was a good friend of Mother's, and they often visited each other.

The phone rang. I ran to answer it. "Hello," I said politely. "Yes, m'am, she's right here. Just a minute, please," I said into the receiver. "Mama," I called, "it's for you."

"Yes, baby," she almost squealed, rushing over taking the phone.

I headed toward the front door; Delores and Sister behind me. We went out to sit on the porch. "What do you want to be when you grow up?" Delores asked.

"I'm going to be a cowboy and ride a horse, just like Roy Rogers."

"You can't be like Roy Rogers, Doris. He's a boy. I mean, he's a man." Sister toyed with me.

"No, for real, I want to be a teacher, like Mother."

"Me too," Sister put in. "I've always wanted to be one since I was little."

"Sister, you're still little," I told her, laughing. "What about you, Delores?" I asked.

"A nurse. That's what the women in my family become, seems like. Both my aunts, my mother. Later, me." She laughed.

"The ladies in my family all seem to be teachers," I said. "Mother, Aunt Kazie, Uncle Leroy, Daddy's brother. Let's play school. We could let the steps be the different grades," I suggested.

"We'd only have third grade, then." Sister laughed.

"I know," I put my bet in two cents in.

"We can put pebbles on the steps to stand for grades. Like this one pebble here means fourth grade. Two pebbles, fifth grade. Three pebbles, sixth, and on until twelfth," she explained, red in the face.

"Does this include college, too?" I asked.

"We don't have enough time, I don't think," Delores said, laughing. We played school until Mother came home. Mama was still on the phone when Mother was going into the house.

The three of us girls sat on the living room couch, ready to watch TV. *The Ed Sullivan Show* would come on later that night; right now, there wasn't too much on, except some talk shows and news shows. Who wanted to look at those? Surely not us.

"Girls," Mother called us, "you can come on in now. It's getting late."

We obeyed. First, we put the rock grade markers back on the ground. Then we walked quietly into the house.

"Did you have a nice time with Mrs. Benson?" Mother asked us as we trumped into the kitchen.

"Yes, m'am," we said together.

"Good! Mrs. Sampson said hello to y'all. I told her about your company, little Missy here." She patted Delores's shoulder. Boy, was I going to miss her when she went home. She must have been reading my mind, for she said at that same time, "I'm sure gonna miss you guys when I go home."

I shook my head to agree. "I wish you lived up here," I told her. The evening set in and soon became eight, time for *The Ed Sullivan Show*, which we always watched.

"I hope they have some colored people on tonight," Sister said. Her wish came true, for sure enough the first group on were The Temptations singing "My Girl" and "Ain't Too Proud to Beg." A dog act was on next, followed by a little Chinese girl with two long ponytail plaits who played these hard songs on the piano. A man playing the violin was next. And Elvis Pressley closed the show, singing, "You Ain't Nothing But a Hound Dog." Mama called him Albert Pressley; so did Sister and I, at first.

After the show was over, bath, brush teeth, and put on hairnet time rolled around. Mother ran our bath water and put the bubble bath in. The tub was full of suds, and the water felt just right. We took off our robes and got in the tub, one by one. We played around a little, but not too much because we were so tired from our busy day.

Once we were bathed well enough, we dried off, put on our pajamas, robes, and house shoes and went out to the kitchen where Mama had coconut cake and milk waiting. I gulped mine down quickly, I almost didn't even taste the moist sweetness. The familiar voice of Mama from the kitchen rang out, "Bedtime, girls! Time for bed, time for bed, all you little sleepy heads." She repeated the phrase several times, changing the tune as she went. *So Mama is a poet*, I thought. *Wow! I think I'll write a poem; after all, I am a poet*, I thought to myself.

I'd once told Sister this, but she just laughed. She stopped laughing, though, when I won first place for the poem I wrote about a circus coming to town. Miss Millie had hung it on the bulletin board and let it stay there for a whole week. I'd read it in front of the class, and everybody had clapped and clapped. "I'm gonna be a poet when I grow up," I had told Mama and Mother when I got home with my prize, a blue paper ribbon.

"It's just paper, Doris," Sister had said, teasing me.

But I didn't care. I had won first place. "Mother, tell us a story," I begged, anything to put off going to sleep. Mother told the best stories. "Mother knows some good stories, Delores," I quipped, smiling at Mother.

"All right, girls, just one story and then off to sleep, you girls!" she said. She hesitated, then raised her hands and shut her eyes, and the woman's words brought a dead man back to life to mysteriously kill his wife and bury her under their house.

She stayed there for year after year while he acted like he was so sad. Then one dark rainy night, something scratched on his door. She crept to the door. "Who's out there?" she asked.

"You know who's standing here. You know." The voice had trailed off into the evening mists.

Mother's voice grew louder as she told certain parts, went back down with other parts, and back up with others. It was almost like listening to a one-person choir at church on Sunday morning.

The man had slowly opened the door, which creaked, creaked, creaked. There, standing at the door, was his dead wife, just standing there, bleeding from her neck, holding her severed head in her arms. She was laughing madly, saying, slowly saying, "I've...got...you, Neal... I've...got...you...Neal." Over and over and over. It was a maddening sound, one to drive a body crazy.

This went on each night. When Neal tried to sleep, the knock would come. He'd open the door and hear the voice, slowly saying, "I've...got... you...Neal. I've...got...you...Neal" over and over and over. Eventually, he wasn't able to function well. He stopped going to work, stopped communicating with people. He even stopped going to church on Sundays. He became unhappy and withdrew within himself. He kept hearing the doorbell ring at night. He'd go to the door to find the woman with blood spurting from her neck, holding her severed head in her arms, and saying, "I've...got...you...Neal. I've...got...you...Neal." Over and over and over.

Neal went down in his health by the day. He lost his job, his friends, even his new wife and children. Before anyone knew it, Neal was gone, gone, gone. No one knew where he went. And until this day, the old people say, on any dark and windy, rainy night, you can hear a man's voice rise out of the dark, "I've...got...you...Neal. I've...got...you...Neal." Over and over and over.

"Oh, Mother, that was the best story. You never told us that one before," I exclaimed.

"That's because it's true. Old Neal's still walking around these streets. He can get into your house, too. He especially likes little girls," Mother told us in a creepy tone of voice. Mother didn't have to say anymore except "goodnight, my girls!" She kissed the three of us. "Then don't let old Neal get you!" That was all we needed to hear. Our heads were on the pillow, and at last, we fell asleep. Over in the night, I woke up. *Neal,* I think, *then and there. He's coming to get me.* "That madman's probably at the side door right now," I told myself.

I shook Sister, but she's out cold. I can hear her breathing. I called Delores, but she's asleep, too. I crawled over Sister to get out of bed. Accidentally, I punched Sister's ribs, and she yelled out, "Ouch!"

I cut on the lamp. "Sorry, Sister," I whispered. I saw Delores sound asleep, snoring with her mouth wide open. If I only had a camera. Sister opened her eyes and rubbed them. "What's wrong?" she whispered, lying there like a human rock.

"I'm scared. I've got to go to the bathroom," I whispered, trying hard not to wake Delores. But that was too late, for she was already sitting up in bed.

"Is it morning already?" She laughed, yawning and stretching. "I just went to sleep."

"We all just went to sleep," I wanted to say, but didn't.

I went to the bathroom, then into Mother's room. She was, as they say, "calling the hogs." "Mother, Mother," I whispered, shaking her lightly.

She sat up and cut the lamp on. "What's wrong, Doris? Are you sick?" she asked, sounding scared.

"No, m'am, I'm just, well, just can't go back to sleep. I woke up and—"

"Go to the bathroom," she said, trying to hold back a yawn.

"I did already," I told her.

"Go back to bed, honey," she said. "You've got to be sleepy. I know I am."

"May I sleep with you?" I asked.

She pulled back the covers. "If it's my only means of getting back to sleep, go on and get in. But I mean, you get right to sleep, right now, you hear? It'll be morning before we know it." She kissed my cheek and cut off the light. "Goodnight, sweetheart, see you in the morning."

I fell right to sleep, snug in Mother's arms, secure in the presence of her safety. I slept the rest of the night with the knowledge that Neal or no problems could plague me now. The next moment, or so it seemed, the sun was shining, plates were rattling, and Mama was singing out in the kitchen "Take Me to the Water" loudly and a bit off-key. She liked that song.

I sat up and looked around for Sister and Delores. They were gone. *Oh, no, Neal's got them,* I thought, ready to cry. But I heard soft giggling and talking and sniggling out in the kitchen. It's Sister and Delores! I thought. I got up and went out to the kitchen.

"Wash your hands and faces and brush your teeth. Then you can come to the table and eat." It was Mama's voice. *Oh, boy, was I hungry,* I thought. Mama was stacking pancakes on a plate, Delores's plate, this one farewell morning. A bright sun was beaming through the kitchen window. Already, it felt warm, like the pancakes I would be putting into my mouth.

Birds were out; already, they were serenading the earth. I didn't know who was better, them or Mama, who was still singing that same verse.

The pancakes, as always, were delicious and easy to slide down my throat. I knew Sister and Delores felt the same. We cleared the table after eating and went to make the bed. I didn't know which bed I should make since I'd been in both.

"Doris, why did you get up last night?" Sister asked, puzzling Delores who never even knew I had been awake.

"Oh, I started thinking about the story Mother told us. I thought Neal was coming to get me."

"Aw, Doris, that's just silly, silly. You know that story's made up. It's just make-believe, like fairies." Sister fussed.

Delores joined in. "She's right, you know, Doris. Neal is made up. He's a made-up man, just like Santa Claus."

"But," I struggled with the word, "Santa Claus isn't made up. Santa Claus is real. I saw him one year when I peeped out in the living room window. Nobody knew I was up. I wanted to see. And I did. There he was in his sleigh, packed with toys. I never told anyone, not even Anna Lee. I didn't wanna get laughed at. But I did see him. For real." I was almost out of breath from telling this story. When I finished, they were believing in Santa Claus again, at least Delores was.

"Delores, gather up all your things, now. Look around real good," Mama told her. "Make sure you don't leave anything behind."

"Yes, Mrs. Lowry. I really have had a good time visiting you all. I sure wish I didn't have to leave," Delores said, almost in tears.

"Oh, we're glad you could come, honey," Mama crowed. "Nellie Mae and your mommy were in college together, and they were roommates in college, too. I believe they were in each other's weddings. They're good friends, just like the three of you!"

"Yes, m'am, I know," Delores responded. Sister and I knew our mothers' histories, too. Mother had told us years ago when we were little girls.

"I sure wish I didn't have to leave," Delores told us, refolding her Easter dress and putting it back into her suitcase. Her other stuff, pajamas, robe, slip, shoes, and extra dress and pants were already packed, along with her Sunday socks and shoes. She put her used underwear in a plastic bag, her pocketbook in a part that zipped.

"I wish you lived up here," I said to her." "We could go to the same school, have the same friends, same teachers, even. We could walk to the library together, sit together in church, and have lots of fun every day, not just during Easter vacation."

"Doris," Sister broke in, "you're just wishing. Delores can't stay here. She has to stay with her mommy and her brothers and father. Don't you think they'd miss her? Be sad if she lives up here?"

"But they'd live up here, too." I defended my cause. "It would be good."

"Yep," Sister agreed, "I imagine it would."

"I'm gonna cry," I told them, wiping a tear with my finger.

"Don't cry, Doris," Delores said, wiping her own tear. "We'll get together again soon."

"I sure hope so," I told her, trying to smile.

The bed was made; the suitcase all packed and shut. It was hair time. Delores and Sister did their own. Mother would have to do mine. Sister still had curls, and Delores had a ponytail. I didn't know how Mother would fix mine. I hoped she'd give me a ponytail like my friend.

"Doris," Mother called, "bring the comb, brush, and Vaseline, and a towel, and come on so I can get you out of the way." I did as she'd said. Immediately, I started squirming as soon as she started in my hair.

"Now, girl," she chided, "you've got to hold still. I'm not hurting you!" She rubbed some Vaseline on and combed it through to the ends. "How do you want it fixed? Two plaits or a ponytail?" she asked, something she didn't usually do. I can't remember her ever giving me a hair choice. I probably would never get one again, either, ever in my life.

Let me go for it. "Fix it in a ponytail, just like Delores's, my good friend."

The Ghost on Miller Street

IT WAS SOMETHING LIKE A sheet—white, flimsy—but wasn't. Something like a dog's howl when rain fell the first autumn night, but wasn't. It was just something else—something Mama couldn't quite put her foot on, something Mother couldn't name.

It was something that came and played in my dreams and tickled Sister's foot, making her think it was me.

"Stop, Doris!" she called out from under the quilt.

I'd turned over, sleepy, dazed. "Stop what?" I'd yawned. "You know, you're crazy, Sister. Go back"—I yawned—"to sleep, will you!"

This time, it was my foot. "Stop, Sister!" I squealed. "Quit tickling my foot and go back to sleep!" I snapped.

A week ago, Mother had made us sleep in our own room. I liked the arrangement. No more hearing Mother snore or feel her cold feet on mine.

Just as soon as I'd settled back in for a good, good sleep, I felt Sister tickle my foot again. "Sister, will you stop! Please. I'm sleepy."

"I'm not bothering you. Now, go to sleep."

"Let's cut on the lamp," I whispered in the dark room.

"You know we can't. Mother said so."

"We'd better get to sleep, Sister," I said as softly as I could. We pulled the quilt up to our necks, cozy-like, happy to have no more disturbances that particular night.

The next morning at breakfast, Sister and I both knew something strange had happened during the night, though neither of us brought it up.

The next night when we were in bed, we heard cows mooing in the street; when we creeped to the window to look, there wasn't anything to see. We heard singing yet saw no people to sing. We even heard horses trotting but saw none in the street.

We thought it was strange, but we didn't say so. "Who had been singing?" we asked each other, to ourselves. Where had the horses come from? Who had brought them? Where were they now? We wondered about these notions, serious as they were.

The next couple of nights were peaceful, quiet. Then, out of nowhere, bells rang, cats meowed, and dogs howled. They seemed to have practiced. They seemed to take turns. They were even in sync, in harmony. And their sounds had been most soothing, gentle and soft, almost like a lullaby.

It would start up around midnight and wear on sometimes for hours. Sometimes it seemed short and abrupt. But it was always there, playing those strange, wild notes.

Mama and Mother had not heard anything and were sure we hadn't either. "You girls were just dreaming." Mother was sure. "That's all it was," Mama had added, "just a dream."

It was no dream! It was as real as anything, like a bed, a rocking chair, or an elm tree in the fall, I wanted to say. Surely, Sister and I wouldn't have had the same identical dreams, seeing the same images in our sleep. It didn't happen the next night or the next several nights. In fact, for a week or two, Sister and I slept soundly from the time we closed our eyes until the next morning. Our dreams were sweet, or at least mine were.

But the one night when it rained, bells started ringing and whistles started blowing, all happening out in the street. Sister heard it, for she woke me up; we both stumbled to the side door, through the dark with just the street light, peeping through the curtains. There was nothing at all out there.

As soon as we got back in bed, the noises started up again, going on until a faint sun came easing into the room. I yawned. I felt so tired like I hadn't slept in weeks.

The next night, the noises in the street started up.

"Did you hear anything last night, Mother?" I asked with a mouth full of buttered toast.

"Not a thing, dear heart." She thought for a moment. "Like what?" she asked.

"Like bells ringing and whistles blowing. Sister heard it too. Out in the middle of the street."

"Aw, girls, you were dreaming, I tell you," Mother exclaimed, alarmed. "You've mentioned this before. You're dreaming, I tell you, dreaming, And talking about it just makes it worse."

"Yes, m'am," I gave in, knowing what it hadn't been—a dream like Mother said.

Sister and I never really found out what we'd heard. We still wondered what had made the sounds, but we were never, ever to know.

And to this very day, when the sun sinks low in the western sky, though Sister resides in Houston, Texas, I, still in the house I grew up in, ask my sixty something self, "All those years ago, when Sister and I were in bed trying to get some sleep, what was making those strange, loud noises?" I never get an answer, though.

The Man Who Jumped
One Morning

THE FRONT DOORBELL RANG—*DING-DONG, DING-DONG, ding-dong!* It was early. I knew it was Mrs. Holly coming to see Mama.

"Mrs. Lara, Mrs. Lara! Did you hear? I was just getting ready to eat my cornflakes.

"No, Mrs. Holly," Mama answered, "hear what?"

"They say James Meyers had a suitcase, called up a Blue Boy taxicab." She stopped short. She was trying to whisper but was so pumped up, she got louder and louder.

Mama, happily listening, hadn't really noticed me pouring my cornflakes, but she finally said, "Doris, go outside!"

"But, Mama, it's too hot to go outside. Besides, I'm starving."

"Let's go sit on the couch," Mama suggested. "It's cool in there, and we can talk better."

The women left, not realizing that I could hear quite well what they said from the kitchen. I crunched my cornflakes, anxious to hear what had happened.

"Yes, they say he put that suitcase in the trunk, got in the taxicab, and had Frog to drive out to the Columbia River. And they say when they got out there, he paid the fare, got out, got his suitcase, and you know, Mrs. Lara..." she slowed up, out of breath. "They say that man jumped in that river. He's gone. Mrs. Lara, dead. And he got that wife and them two children. I forget what they names is.

That girl might near Doris's age, and the boy, he round Vera's age. Lord, what *is* they go do?"

Well, I had the story now. I knew that family, too. Jamey Jr. and I were in a band together. He played the saxophone.

We never did find out why a healthy man who looked that good would jump into muddy water early on a summer morning, a man who had a boy and girl and a pretty wife.

"Sometimes things will happen. They just go wrong, and we don't know why," Mother had said over dinner.

"Mother," I asked, really wanting to know, "does it hurt when you jump into a lake?"

"Finish your dinner, Doris." That's the only thing she said. From her look, I knew I'd better start back eating.

The Girl Who Had Three Dresses and Two Pairs of Shorts

S HE CAME TO OUR SCHOOL one rainy March morning, her notebooks in worn purple satchel, her lunch in a soggy brown paper bag. She had rough-looking skin that I was sure Blue Seal Vaseline could fix right up. Mama and Mother swore by Blue Seal Vaseline, smearing it on their faces every night and putting it in Sister and my hair when they combed it every morning. Even her name sounded wrong or least different—we'd never heard it before; at least, not until now. Hortense Ann Flogg.

Maybe we could call her Ann, I thought. But at short recess, when we girls got in our huddle to laugh and talk a bit, this new girl joined us. Before we dispersed, it was apparent what she would be called—Hortense.

Hortense took the weekly spelling test. Mrs. Ridder would always call the names of the students who'd made 90 or above. She called four names: Sonny Boy's, mine, Hortense's and Shirley's. At least, I thought, if Hortense wasn't that pretty, she sure was smart.

The days wore on; cool mornings became warm ones. Eventually, we girls could start wearing shorts if they weren't too short. But Hortense kept wearing those same three dresses she always wore.

One day during short recess, I whispered to her, "Why don't you ever wear shorts?"

"I don't have any shorts, just dresses," she whispered back.

"Can you come home with me tomorrow?"

"I'll have to ask my mama." She smiled.

We had an English test later that day. As always, we exchanged papers. I made an A, and so did Hortense. I thought the test was easy. We'd had to name the parts of speech and give their definitions. We even had an oral part. One by one, we had to get up in front of the class and name the part of speech the teacher said in the sentence.

Johnny Simpson, the tallest boy in the class went up. He seemed to loom over everything—the desks, the blackboard, even the teacher's desk. Mrs. Ridder said the sentence, "The boat rowed down the river." She asked with expectancy, her eyes wide. She waited. "What's the verb?"

Johnny thought, put his hand on his chin, looked up, then out of us looking at him. "The verb in this sentence is *down*," he answered. He looked around, proud that he knew he hit the answer on the head, getting it correct. But though Johnny was a sports star, he was not too good in his schoolwork.

Mrs. Rudder, not wanting to give up on Johnny, urged, "Johnny, now just think, can you *down*?"

Johnny thought for a second. He looked at the ceiling, the bookcase, the blackboard, out at us looking at him. Then he gave his answer with deep faith that it was right, "Yes, m'am." He smiled widely. "I can set *down*!"

We all looked at each other, knowing he was wrong, and trying not to laugh.

Mrs. Ridder, being kind and experienced at this, just said gently, "No, Johnny, the verb is *rowed*. I suggest you study your list when you go home."

We continued the exercise until everyone had had a turn.

Hortense came home with me the next couple of days. We played Jacks; I won two games, and she won four. "What's your favorite game," I asked her.

She seemed to think, as if not having one. Then she said, "I don't really know.' She stood, put her hands on her hips, and said with a giggle, "You know, I like playing Checkers. That's my favorite game. I like playing Hide-and-Seek too and Ring around the Rosie."

"Yeah, me too. What about Little Sally Walker?" I asked.

"Little Sally Walker? Is that a game?" She seemed puzzled, out of sorts, like a lost dog. We were learning about similes and metaphors, and I guessed she wanted to sound smart.

"I suppose," I told her, "just like the other games. You know, Punch-a-Nella." We sat back down on the steps, playing Jacks, laughing and talking for the longest.

Sister came home, carrying a stack of library books, all about science. She had been talking about doing a report on an animal the teacher picked. Her animal was the tiger.

I called Sister over to the corner, whispering, "She doesn't have any shorts. Could you give her a pair of yours and a top? You're about the same size."

Sister looked at my friend and giggled. "Do I look like Tots and Teens?" With that, I knew she would.

Sister, still holding her library books, told us she'd be back as soon as she put them down. She came back and led Hortense and me to our room where she pulled out two pairs of last year's shorts. I knew because I had some just like them; Mother often bought us clothes just alike.

"Here you go," Sister told Hortense as she handed over the shorts. "You can try them on in there," she told her, pointing to the bathroom.

Hortense came out with the shorts on, smiling broadly. "Thank you so much!" she beamed at Sister. She had the other set in her hands tightly, almost scared that we'd take them back from her. "I just know the others will fit," she added, as if to make sure Sister would let her have them before she tried them on.

The next day in school, Hortense wore her new short set, the one she hadn't tried on. She had on white socks and tennis shoes and seemed proud as anything. At short recess, she got very close to my ear, whispering into it, "Thanks again, Doris. I love my new shorts. I love my new friend too, you." She laughed.

Later that day, we had a spelling test. We exchanged papers to correct the tests. Afterward, when Mrs. Ridder had checked them over, she called out some names, first names only, and the grades: Sonny Boy, 90; Hortense, 100, and Doris, 95. The next day, I found out that Ramona had made 85, and she hadn't even cheated like she had one other time, getting caught. Mrs. Ridder had given her five licks in her hand with that big black strap she kept in her desk drawer. Ramona had tried hard not to cry, but she did. We didn't know whether it was from hurt or from shame.

Hortense stayed at school the remainder of that spring. When we came back the next year, she was not there. We wondered about her, where she was, the girl who made good grades, who wore three dresses on three different days, and two short sets in late spring. But we just wondered with questions that had no apparent answers.

More Than Just the Twist

"**C**OME ON, BABY, AND LET'S do The Twist." Chubby Checker's magic words sent me out on the dance floor, unashamed at last. For since I could remember, the girls had declared as we played and moved to our forty-five records, "Doris can't dance!" I thought they were right, too, for a while, though I was doing the same side swooshing that they did. At home, I got out the record player and played "The Twist," and when no one was watching, except my doll, I did The Twist. When the record had finished playing, I still heard it inside my head, and I still did "The Twist."

So at Ethel Lee Armstrong's eleventh birthday party, she played records. We girls danced when "The Twist" came on. I danced too. I even came in second when she held a Twist contest. "When I grow up," I told myself, "I'm going to be a dancer, just like Chubby Checker!" I meant that too, for a while anyway, until something else entered my ten-year-old brain, and I'd want to be something else.

I was out in the front yard, humming "The Twist" while making the dance motions when Mama's friend, Mrs. Harris, stepped into the yard. "Hey, Doris, Mrs. Lara in the house?" She always messed up Mama's name. I wanted to correct her—Low-Ry—but I just shook my head, smiled, and answered, "Yes, m'am." She went in.

Before long, I could hear the women laughing from in the house, probably about something Mrs. Harris had said about Charley, her son-in-law. She could not stand Charley, and she didn't try to hide it. I went back to twisting, but not for long. Soon after, Mama called me into the house, "Doris, come play a piece for Mrs. Harris!" She was proud of my playing and jumped at every chance to get me to play for someone, anyone.

"Aw, Mama, Mrs. Harris don't wanna hear no piano playing."

But Mama threw her eye, catapulting me over to the piano stool. "Watch your language, child," she said.

"What would you like to hear, Mrs. Harris?" I asked politely, cutting my eyes at Mama, who seemed pleased at last.

"Just anything, darling," she answered.

I flexed my fingers. Needing no music book because I played by ear, I first played "What a Friend We Stand in Jesus."

"Oh, that was lovely, baby," she laughed. "Now, play something else.

I obliged and played "Just As I Am," "Jesus Keep Me Near the Cross," and "Jesus Paid It All" all in a row, one by one. Both the women were smiling as I finished up my little concert. Mama, proud, beaming and in a jubilant mood, offered, "Come on in the kitchen." She nodded to her friend. "and have some cake." Mrs. Harris followed, smiling. I did too. But Mama turned me around. "You've got to eat your dinner first," she scoffed.

I wandered back outside, when I switched from my hymn mode back to Rock 'n' Roll, particularly "The Twist," my favorite. I started the rhythmic song once again inside my head, "Come on, baby, and let's do The Twist!" Cool, energized, boldly, with no one around to look, I did "The Twist" right in the front yard, with only my doll Donna there to watch.

Music Lessons and
Homemade Wine

WHEN YOU'RE GROWING UP, THERE are just some things you just not ought to do. Run away from home is one. Talk back to an adult is another. And get into your grandmother's homemade grape wine, no matter how sweet the flavor, is the ultimate one.

I had been practicing my piano lesson all afternoon and finally could play the song without looking at the book. Really, I could hear Mr. Brenner play a piece once or twice and already be able to play the song without the book. Mama called it "playing music by ear." Mr. Brenner didn't want the music played like that. He wanted his students to learn how to read music and play notes.

Anyway, on a very warm day in May, a few hours before my music lesson, I was home all by myself. "You can do this for a short while," Mama had said. "You're growing up, getting to be a big girl." And I was. My dress size and shoe size were both bigger, and I was in an upper grade than before.

Well, though I wasn't supposed to have been anywhere near Mama and Aunt Babe, who'd caught a ride and come over to help, I was right there at the door, listening, peeping, hearing words I shouldn't hear.

Anyway, I saw them, Mama and Aunt Babe, wash the purple grapes over, over, and over, then mash them up using their hands, then put them in a curtain, squeeze the juice out into a pot, and put cups of sugar in a pot. They poured it from one pot to the other, from one to the other, one to the other. Then they let it sit, to let the flavor steep through. Once that was done for about an hour, they poured the brew into a boiler and let it steep on the stove for about a half hour. And then, the hot brew was poured into Mason jars and put out on the back porch to cool.

They sampled the purple mixture with teaspoons, their expressions declaring its goodness.

"I think this is our best we ever made, Babe. We haven't made wine in a couple of years," Mama said.

"That's right, Venie, and when we did, we gave it all away."

"Not this time, Babe, we'll keep a few jars for ourselves." And they had. Aunt Babe had carted hers off when her ride picked her up, and Mama had stored three jars in the lower cabinet, after giving Anna Lee's mother two and Mrs. Helms three. Mama and Aunt Babe could have gone into the wine business for themselves.

I knew where Mama had stored her wine, and so, on this very warm May afternoon, as I waited to go for my piano lesson, I decided to help myself to a glass of that good tasting liquid Aunt Babe and Mama called wine.

I got a breakfast glass and twisted the cap off the Mason jar, which went *whish, pop*! Some spilled out and ran down the side of the cabinet, dripping down onto the floor.

The purple stuff in the glass tasted so sweet, so good that I gulped it down, in big swallows, stopping only to breathe and lick my lips. I repeated this until the glass was empty, the liquid gone. Just like that!

All of a sudden, the kitchen started to spin, going round and round in such urgency that I found myself stretched on the floor.

Mama and Aunt Babe

I can't remember how long I lay on the floor, only that I jumped up, startled at the sound of Mother and Mama's voices coming back from the store.

Mother's voice called, "Doris, get your music book and come on out to the car. You don't want to be late for your lesson."

When I got up, the room was circling, making me dizzy. I grabbed the counter to keep from falling.

"Doris," Mother called again, "come on, now! Quit dragging your heels. You're going to be late, and you know that man doesn't like it when you're late."

I could barely stay on my feet. The room was spinning, and I with it. My head hurt, my stomach was churning, but I knew I had to go.

I stumbled into the living, fumbled in the piano stool for my music books, and went that same way out to the car. Maybe I wouldn't feel the pain of Mr. Brenner's cane if I hit a wrong note today, feeling like I'm feeling now.

Maybe Mr. Brenner wouldn't notice if I hit a wrong note. Maybe he'd have been drinking his "special drink" as he called it before practice even started: four o'clock, sharp. "Doris, did you put on deodorant?" Mother asked as I got out of the car to go into Mr. Brenner's.

When I got there, two other girls were already waiting. One was playing. I could hear the sour notes as I walked—sideways—into the parlor. I could hear the whacks, the sniffles, already. Then mixing in with my queasy stomach and swimming head didn't make such a good combination.

"Ezell, you're about to be late! You know you don't come in my practice sessions late! No, no!"

"Yes, sir," I mumbled, trying hard not to be heard. He was in rare form today, something I did not need in my life.

"Speak up! What did you say? I couldn't hear you," he pushed.

"I didn't say anything, Mr. Brenner," I answered, slurring my words, holding my stomach. The smell of that wine came up out of my stomach like a car on the racetrack, filling up the parlor. Yuck!

Patricia and Aliene noticed it, for they started fanning with their music books. "What've y'all been doing?" I asked, my hand over my mouth trying to cover the wine smell.

"Oh, nothing much, just school and homework, and stuff," Patricia answered.

"Yeah," Aliene put in. "And stuff."

"What kind of stuff?" I asked, my head and stomach still churning, still jumping. I barely made it back to the bathroom before my whole stomach seemed to be coming back up. I got one of the bath cloths hanging from the sink and mopped my face and neck, then the floor where I had gone.

I scooped water into my mouth with my hand and gargled, spitting into the sink. I wiped my face dry with the towel hanging down. Then I went stumbling back to join the girls.

I remember starting to out talk my thoughts. I asked Patricia and Aliene questions and gave my thoughts about the answers before either of them could speak. I talked about what I had done that day and about my plans for the next day. I talked about how my summer would be spent, though what I thought I had said was nothing but pure fiction, since neither Mother nor Mama had even mentioned summer yet.

"Anderson! You're next!" Mr. Brenner called in his strict, matter-of-fact tone of voice.

Patricia got up, looked back at us sadly, like her puppy had just died, and went to the piano.

"What's your favorite subject?" I asked Aliene. "Oh, mine is English, and I absolutely *hate* math!" I went on and on, not giving Aliene a chance to say anything in response.

Then I got up and started to dance around and around in the parlor, laughing wildly. Aliene called out to me. I think it was she. Or at least I think it was Aliene. I didn't really know because I was still a bit foggy from that wine.

I'd heard several sour notes come from the piano, followed by whacks on fingers, Patricia's.

Oh, oh, I thought through my fuzzy brain. He's in that mood for beating fingers. If only I could get hold of that cane. I had just finished my wild dance around the parlor with Patricia watching with wide eyes my every move when Mr. Brenner called, "Skinner!" Adding, "Anderson, make sure you practice that piano. A lot!"

"Yes, sir, I will. *A lot!*" she mimicked, her back turned.

Mr. Brenner would advise Aliene to practice "a lot" too, for as soon as she started to play, sour notes came up from the piano. Maybe Mr. Brenner needed to have that piano tuned, I thought.

"I just feel like dancing!" I said, standing up, twirling around in place and knocking a vase of flowers over. It went crashing to the floor, pieces of glass going all over the carpet.

Oh, oh, I thought, *I'm in big trouble now!* Mr. Brenner came out, a big frown on his face. "What's going on out here? Who's tearing up my house this time? Say! Ezell!" He looked dead at me, knowing my history for making past mischief.

"Oh, Mr. Brenner," I cried, "I promise, it was an accident! I didn't mean to break your vase. I swear I didn't."

"And swearing on top of it. You know you know better." He howled.

Tears, from fright, from pain, from the unknown because I didn't know what awaited me, though I knew it would be bad, trickled down my face and dropped into my lap. My fingers stretched out to catch them.

"I'm so sorry, Mr. Brenner. I didn't mean it," I pleaded. "Pl-e-a-se don't tell my mama. She'll give me a whipping, for sure!"

"You better hope I don't give you one first!" he hollered. "You been actin' up ever since you got here. You know y'all supposed to sit down and hush your mouths out in this parlor. That's the rules! Miss Doris Ezell!"

"Yes, sir." I wept, trying to sound like my friend had died. "But I didn't mean to break your vase, honest!" The room, plus Mr. Brenner hollering at me, spun me around now. My stomach was churning. I felt hot, faint. My face flushed, my nose ran. I sucked up the hot mucus still in my nostrils.

"Ezell," he snorted out something that I couldn't quite make out. Then, "When I get through in here and get ready for you, you better know every note on that page!" He was so mad, he was spitting when he said *page*.

My head was splitting, and every word he said made it split open a little wider. He finished up with Aliene pretty quickly, seemingly eager to get to me. I was so scared, I thought I had forgotten my song. I swallowed my gum, which I was not supposed to have anyway.

"Ezell!" Mr. Brenner shouted. "Come on. And you better not miss a note today, not one note!"

I was ready. I played the notes on the page and songs I remembered hearing. I played songs I'd heard in church, on the radio. I even played songs I'd heard Mama humming and Mother singing. I didn't know how or why. Today was the day I decided to play by ear. Wrong day, wrong choice. He was not in the mood, though I put on quite the show, playing tune after tune after tune, and all by ear.

My head was still hurting and felt like it was going on a swim. I heard myself talking while my fingers were playing. And I was laughing at nothing and could not stop. Nothing and everything seemed funny.

Sister had come in. Sitting in the parlor, she seemed like two people looking in at me. She looked so funny, and I didn't know why. I waved at her like she was a stranger from out of town. The miniconcert ended, and Mr. Brenner looked down at me, shaking his head, a half grin on his face.

"Ezell," he said, "next week, you all have three songs, pages 33, 34, and 36. And no more monkey business either. I'm gonna tell Mrs. Lowry how you acted today. As soon as I see her, I'm telling!" He promised. With every word he said, it played a note in my head.

I was still wobbly when I walked and bumped into the parlor wall before plopping down on the couch. Patricia giggled, but Sister just glared at me.

"Ezell," Mr. Brenner called.

"I finished already," I blurted out.

"I mean Vera," he corrected.

"Oh, hey, Sister." I grinned. "When did you come?"

"Doris." It's all she said as she walked over to the piano like we'd never met.

"I'm in a big-time trouble," I told Patricia who waited for her ride.

"Maybe not," she said, trying to comfort me.

"You don't know my grandmother and mother. They'll kill me. Ouch. My head hurts so bad." I groaned.

"That's it!" she offered. "Just tell 'em you got a real bad headache."

"I do, you know. How did you do with your lesson today?"

"All right, I guess. At least he didn't hit me." She laughed.

"Yeah, me neither. That's always the test, isn't it?" We both laughed. The room looked green.

A car horn blew outside. Patricia jumped up. "I think that's my mom. See you next week, Doris. Practice, practice, practice!" she teased. It's what Mr. Brenner always told us.

I didn't hear Sister play any wrong notes. But then, she never played wrong notes. Her fingers never got beat. She practiced at home and got her lessons right, all the time.

She finished up and came into the parlor where I was. Sandra, Mr. Brenner's younger sister who was deaf, must have cleaned up the broken vase for only a tiny piece was still on the rug. "Very good lesson, Ezell!" he called.

"Watch out, Sister," I warned. "There's broken glass."

"Doris." She inhaled, "What have you done now?" We laughed and waited for Mother to come pick us up.

"Sister, my head still hurts," I moaned.

"Oh, Doris, you'll be okay. We'll be home soon, and you can lie down," she soothed. Somehow, Sister always knew just the right thing to say.

A couple of weeks later, we had our spring concert. Mr. Brenner talked to Mama and Mother afterward and mentioned my behavior that fated day when I acted up.

When Mama explained that I had gotten into the homemade wine, he held his head back laughing so hard, I thought he would burst.

"Oh, Mrs. Lowry, that's okay. The only thing I hate about that is she didn't bring me some."

The next piano practice, I took Mr. Brenner a brown paper bag with a Mason jar full of purple liquid, the same I'd had just a couple of weeks before.

When Pain Turned Navy Purple

"DORIS, YOU BE CAREFUL WHEN you ride that bike!" They had cautioned me over and over, time and again. So when I went flying into the sweet summer air, head first with nothing but air to frame me, to cushion me, I couldn't help but feel the hard, gravely pavement. It was right there, no other place to be, and my ten-year-old backside had taken it all in. I felt the hot liquid drain through my shorts.

Little did I know the damage that was done as I hurried to get up, pretending not to be hurt, but crying anyway, rather from shame than the hurt building in my right leg. I really couldn't tell right off, but I feared my leg was broken. All I could do was wait to find out.

I limped and hobbled around. I couldn't really bend my leg or straighten it out or put all of my weight down on it when I walked. And it was getting big around my knee and was getting all red.

"What's wrong with Doris's leg?" Sister asked Mama and Mother, pointing them to my bangled leg, waiting for them to take turns fussing.

"I told you to be careful on that bike, didn't I?" Mama would probe. "You had no business with a bike anyway!" she would add.

But why? I thought, daring to keep it inside my head. *All my friends have bikes,* I thought, keeping that also inside my head.

Boy. What I would love to say if only I could, and if Mama could have read my thoughts, I'd be a ding dong dead girl. So I just kept still, shook my head and shoulders, and escaped to the next phase, a sweet daydream about a handsome prince who'd swoop down and get me. No time to get involved with what didn't really matter.

My leg was really hurting me now. It was as if the pain had grown a monster's face and was growling, snarling, barking, and foaming at the mouth, a rabid monster with poison-filled fangs in place of teeth. The fangs bit into my tender ten-year-old flesh, pulling it, pawing at it, clawing at it until the flesh came loose.

The pain was getting worse. I had hopped on my good leg up the sidewalk, hoping to beat Mama home. No luck. She had just come in from her garden and had just started dusting. She hadn't known something was wrong until Sister had pointed it out to them both.

Tears were running down my face. I mopped them with the back of my hand. The pain was throbbing now, navy purple, on the outside of my leg, or so it seemed.

Uncle Sonny had hurt like this, he'd said, before they cut off his leg. Maybe Dr. Dearheart was going to cut off my leg, too. Boy, was I hurting and scared, nervous and shaking. "We've got to get her to the doctor, fast!" It was Mother, frantic, panting, tears starting up. Mama came rushing out of the bedroom where she'd been dusting. She didn't even take off her apron.

Mother helped me hop on my good leg out to the car. She carefully put me on the back seat, stretching out my hurt leg on the seat. Sister squeezed in beside me, careful not to get on my burning, aching leg.

The drive to Dr. Dearheart's office seemed to take a year, but at last, we were there. Mother hurriedly whisked me unto my good leg and helped me to the stairs. She scooped me up in her arms, carrying me up the steps. At other times, Sister would have teased me, chanting, "Doris is a baby, Doris is a baby." Not today. She had a pained look on her face that let me know she was quite worried about her little sister.

Mother helped me into the waiting room where we were greeted by Nurse Kimble. She was dressed in all white, even her funny-looking cap. Everybody else sat on the long green couch, except me.

"Mrs. Ezell," Nurse Kimble finally said, "you can bring Doris on back." Mother, Mama, and I followed her; Mother on one side of me, Mama on the other. They lifted me up on the table.

"Well, young lady," Dr. Dearheart said, who was always laughing, no matter how sick you were. "What seems to be your trouble?"

"I fell off my bike and hurt my leg. Are you going to cut it off?" I blubbered, unable to hold back the tears.

He laughed and wiped my tears with a Kleenex tissue. "Now, Doris, why do you think I would ever cut off your leg? You couldn't play ball or chase your boyfriend!" He laughed. I was trembling from pain, from the fright of it all, the whole day even, that had started out with pancakes and syrup—so good.

"They cut off my Uncle Sonny's leg when he broke it."

"And how do you know," he joked, "you ever broke your leg? It could just be just a big bee sting!"

"Dr. Dearheart." I giggled through a sharp shoot of pain. I whispered, "I am scared."

"Let's take a look here. Get some film of her leg," he directed to Nurse Kimble. They took several pictures, twisting my leg this way and that. It hurt, but I kept still.

I wanted to scream, cry out. But I held it in and took the pain, hot, searing, mean. Waiting for the film to come to light, all I could do was lie there, think and weep. I thought about Anna Lee, what she might say when she found out.

Dr. Dearheart came back out, carrying several films and wearing a grim face. He tried to sound cheery when he gave Mother the news. "It is a break," he told her frankly. "But it's a clean hairline fracture of the tibia. She's young. She'll heal fast. We'll cast it, and she'll be running around again in about six short weeks." He looked over at me, saying, "What do you think about that?"

I wanted to tell him what I was thinking at the time, but Sister and I weren't supposed to use "bad" words.

"Nurse, assist," he ordered as he got ready to set my leg. "This is going to sting. I have to give you several shots in your leg." He pulled my leg, then jerked it one way and then another. With each way he turned it, I yelped. I couldn't help it. It hurt.

I watched as Dr. Dearheart and Nurse Kimble wrapped stuffed white cotton up and down my leg. They positioned it and then wrapped wet, white gauze stripes around my whole leg, only leaving my toes out.

Doris in Her Cast

Six weeks is a long, long time. I couldn't ride my bike. I couldn't skip up and down the paved street. I couldn't run around in our grassy, front yard, seeing who was faster, Anna Lee or me.

But what I could do was watch TV while lying on the couch, play with my paper dolls, read my book *The Bobsey Twins*. Maybe these six weeks wouldn't be so bad. Plus, I would have no chores. Things were looking up.

Dr. Dearheart and Nurse Kimble finished their work. He talked to Mother about my medicine and care. I felt sure ice cream was in this deal. And later on, I found out, as I was helped in dressing for bed, that I was right! The proof was in the bowl: mine, chocolate; Sister's, butter pecan.

And the six long weeks ended being just that—pain endured for six long weeks!

When Bobby Sherman Died,
So Did Some of Us

I DIDN'T CRY WHEN I GOT the sad news that he'd drowned, but I did remember how well Bobby Sherman had played his trumpet. I remembered how we'd have to go down the line, each person playing one at a time until told to stop. I'd seem to always hit a few misplaced notes on the bells. Mr. Banks seemed to stop me pretty early, earlier than anybody else, or so I thought.

But Bobby always sounded like he was doing a concert. Mr. Banks let him play sometimes the whole song. We all would love it and would just smile, wishing we could play that well.

I remember one day as we waited outside for Mr. Banks to open up the band room, I saw Bobby watching me. Since he was older, the unwritten rule said he couldn't talk to me. But it didn't say he could look, smile. And smile he did—all needed to melt my eleven-year-old heart.

And so it continued. One day as I was leaving Mr. Gibson's store, I spotted Bobby walking with some boys on the other side of the street. They were laughing and talking together. Their voices were muffled, but loud enough, enough for me to hear one say, "That's Doris Ezell." I got a little frightened, for boys didn't usually walk over our way this time of day.

I just grinned and waved, saying, "Hi, Bobby. I'll see you at band practice."

He had smiled that cute, crooked smile, and he laughed, waved and had said, "Hi, Doris, see you in band practice!" Actually, he had winked at me. We went on our ways; my heart actually pounding.

I didn't tell anybody that Bobby Sherman had winked his eye at me, that he'd waved and spoken to me. Boy, oh boy, but was I happy! Band practices became something I itched for, just couldn't wait to happen. I knew that Bobby knew I, at least, was in the world, that I existed.

One afternoon in spring, as we all stood around waiting for Mr. Banks, I caught Bobby looking at me from the corner of his eye. If I had been butter, I'd have melted. When we were walking into the band room, his hand brushed up against mine. Accidentally or on purpose? I might never know.

When school was finally out, some things continued. Mr. Banks still held practices and took us on long daily walks, way down in Sunset View, up Horton Street, back to Clayton Road. We got hot, tired, sweaty. Some of our sneakers, like mine, got holes in them. But our legs got strong from those long walks. They got sturdy, well-balanced.

Bobby even marched well, if that could even happen, but he always did. When we were in the Christmas parade, the trumpet section marched in front of the flutes and bells. I could look dead at Bobby, seeing him lift his legs so perfectly up and down, placing them just right. I had been so busy watching him, I'd almost gotten out of step myself.

That had been the last parade that Bobby had marched in. That following summer, he had gone swimming with his friends. He'd caught a cramp in his leg, gone down into the water to never come up ever again. Forever is a long, long time, and that's how long I will remember Bobby Sherman, the cute boy who blew his trumpet really, really well.

I didn't know Bobby Fisher too well. Only that we were in band together. He played a trumpet; I, the bells. I knew he had a brother and two sisters who were tall. They lived in a white house not too far from us. I knew that he was cute, and one day, he went swimming but never came home.

Word got back to Miller Street fast. The women had been standing out, finished with their housework, supper on the stoves. They still wore their aprons. Mrs. Anderson came rushing down the street, sweat pouring down her face. She seemed frantic, and later we found out what she'd said.

"Bobby Sherman got drowned!" she reported. "A car full of teenagers went swimming at the lake. He caught a cramp, went under, and just drowned. They say they tried to save him, but it was just too late. That poor boy died, just died. He's dead."

And that was how the news came.

Sister and I were very sad. He was the first young person we knew who had really died. Except that girl whose mama went crazy and hit her in the head with a frying pan, over and over and over. Mr. Banks, our band leader, took up a collection and bought flowers to send to Bobby's people. In summer band, some of the girls cried as the big plate was passed around.

And to this very day, the old folks say, if you go out to the river on a very hot day, you can still see Bobby Sherman walking and hear him blowing his trumpet.

When A Rock Hit Me in the Head

WHEN YOU'RE A KID, THERE are some things you just want to forget. Major, intense, excruciating pain is one of them, along with the cause.

I was in the sixth grade, and our class was out for a short recess. My friends and I stood under the big oak tree, like we always did, singing a song we'd learned in third grade. It was about leaves turning colors and falling from trees in the fall. It was a cute song, but our lack in musical talent did that song no justice.

Out of nowhere, the rock, full force, smashed the left side of my head. My legs trembled, went numb, and weren't there anymore. I went sprawling onto the ground, blood spurting from my head.

Dazed, I just lay there, unable to do anything but cry. My head felt like a freight train was trudging through it. I felt something wet on my head—blood.

By this time, my friends had pulled Mrs. Benton over. I heard one of them call, "Come quick, Mrs. Benton, Doris Ezell's dead. A big old rock took and hit her in the head."

A crowd had gathered around me. Mrs. Benton shooed them away. She told me not to move my head. She sent a student to get the school nurse.

Blood had streamed out of my head like an ever-flowing fountain. It had soaked my white blouse. The pain was shooting now, burning red and hot. I had never felt like this before.

"Mrs. Benton," it was Patricia's panicked voice, "is Doris dead?"

Mrs. Benton had to laugh in spite of it all. She answered, "No, Patricia, Doris is not dead. I see the nurse coming; Doris, but don't move."

The blood still seeped out where the rock had struck. My eye hurts, plus the side of my face. I just knew I was dying and asked Mrs. Benton the question. It even hurt to talk. "Doris, no!" she blasted. "No talking," she added, "you'll only make the pain worse."

The nurse arrived, dressed all in white. She looked like two people carrying two black bags. She knelt down, getting red dust all on her white uniform, and said, "Doris, honey, you're going to be fine. I want to check you out first and get you up to the health room. We've called Mrs. Lowry. She's coming in a taxi to take you to the doctor. Meanwhile, how many fingers am I holding up?" she puffed, holding up a finger.

Gosh, it even hurt to look. Would this pain ever stop? "Two," I answered. I could hear the muffled voices of my friends going by into the school.

"Bye, Doris, hope you feel better," someone called, walking by. "Feel better, dear," Mrs. Benton called as she went by.

"Come on, let's go up to the health room. Let me help you." She put her arm around my back and slowly scooped me up. I was a bit wobbly, and I staggered some more when I walked. The nurse helped me up the stairs into the building.

"My head hurts so bad," I told her.

"We're gonna get you something for that pain," she told me as she helped me into the health room. Mrs. Benton had sent up my satchel up, and it was lying on the bed.

She helped me onto the bed and covered me up. Then she walked over to the metal medicine cabinet, unlocked it, and took out some medicine. She filled up a paper cup with water and brought both to me.

"Here, honey, take this." She reached me the white pill and a flowered paper cup. "Now drink all the water down. This medicine requires a lot of water." I did as I was told. "Now, let's lie down until Mrs. Lowry comes."

"Yes, m'am," I answered, lying back on the soft pillow. "My head still hurts." When I closed my eyes, that even hurt.

I slept for I don't know how long, and I awoke to a gentle tugging and a familiar voice. "Doris, honey, Mama's here," Mama was saying. I opened my eyes, that even hurt. I'd cry if I remembered how. Aw, did my head hurt. I wondered if it would ever stop. "Come on, baby, get up," Mama coached, pulling me up.

"Careful, Mrs. Lowry," the nurse cautioned. "Doris might have a concussion."

"Oh," Mama offered.

I was sure she had no idea what that meant, just like me. The two women got on both sides of me, helping me out to Frog's taxicab. Mama carried my satchel.

"Let her lie on the seat," Nurse Byars recommended. She and Mama lowered my head gently onto the back seat, then propped up my legs. "Mrs. Law said she'll bring Doris's lessons home if she feels like doing them." *Good old Mrs. Law,* I thought.

The ride to Dr. Dearheart's office was a mix of bumpy dirt roads and smooth paved highways. Every bump in the road I felt in my head, and every ding on the street, my head felt.

When we got to Dr. Dearheart's, Frog read the meter and told Mama, "A dollar and fifty cents," and added, "I sho' hope the little lady go be all right. I be saying a prayer for her, Mrs. Lowry."

"Thank you, Frog, "Mama answered. "I'm sure she'll be fine. We just have to let the doctor check her out."

And check me out he did. I had to wiggle my toes and fingers, wave my hands, jump up and down, count from one hundred down to one, and stick out my tongue and say, "Ah." He had me to lie back while he punched my stomach. Finally, he put a solution on a cotton ball and washed where the rock had made contact. It stung. "Now, you'll wash this cut every few hours. Don't put a Band-Aid over it. Just let it air-dry. And get her in to see an eye doctor as soon as possible. Today, if possible, tomorrow at the latest. Her cornea in that left eye is all red. It could have infection in it." He sighed. I thought he was so cute.

"Can you refer us to a good eye doctor, Dr. Dearheart?"

"Dr. Hollis, Mrs. Lowry, is one of the best. I could call and see if he could get you in today. The eye is nothing to play with."

"That'll be fine. I'm sure he takes insurance. Doris is on both Nellie and Stanley's plans."

Here we go again, I thought, as pain seared through my head. The nurse called a taxi, directed him to drive us straight to see Dr. Hollis's office. Dr. Dearheart had gotten us an emergency appointment. We didn't even have to go wait in the colored waiting room.

A nurse was waiting at the door when we arrived at Dr. Hollis's office. She looked hard at me, especially at all the blood on my clothes, matching my red eye.

"My, my," she cackled like a hen, "what happened to you?" She tried to laugh and turn the dire situation into a joke. It didn't quite work, for tears welled up in my eyes and rolled down my cheeks. "There, there, honey," she said, shoving a Kleenex into my hand, "you're going to be just fine. Come on back with me, and let's see the doctor." She led us to a room with a table and big, high armchair in it. She directed me to the chair and pinned a giant baby's bib around my neck.

"*Was the eye doctor going to give me a bottle of milk?*" I asked myself.

"Now you just sit back and relax, little pretty girl." She laughed. "The doctor will be right in." She was kidding. They must've met each other coming and going.

Dr. Hollis practically skipped into the room where Mama and I were. He looked at both of us, grinned and asked, "And which of you girls is the patient?" Then he looked at Mama and poked her stomach, and said, "I'll bet it's you!"

I laughed. "No, Dr. Hollis, I'm the patient. A rock hit me on the side of my head." His eyes grew big, concerned.

"A rock, you say?"

"Yes, sir," Mama reported, "Dr. Dearheart said if it had hit one centimeter in the other direction, Doris would have been fatal."

"Oh, my, my, we couldn't have that, could we?" he asked, shining a light in my right eye, then my left.

"Now, young lady, I'm going to put a few drops in your eyes. It'll sting, but it won't be too bad. I want to take a look at the cornea. Now open your eyes and try to hold still. Don't move." He dropped three drops into each eye slowly, then held a Kleenex to each to catch what drained off.

My eyes were stinging like crazy. I blinked a couple of times. "There," he said, "that wasn't too bad, was it?"

"No, sir," I fibbed, "not too bad, but boy, does my head still hurt!"

"Well, it's probably gonna hurt a good while longer. After all, you did get hit in the head with a rock. Your grandma said your doctor said it could have been a deadly accident."

Mama pitched in, "Yes, Dr. Dearheart said if the rock had hit one centimeter in the other direction, it would have been fatal." I knew Mama would enjoy telling what Dr. Dearheart had said for the longest.

My eyes were stinging and burning like crazy.

"Now, Doris," Dr. Hollis said, holding my right eye open, "let's have a look." He shined the bright light in my eye. "Uh-huh." He did the same with my left eye. "Uh-huh, Doris," he said, sounding satisfied.

"Well, the good news is you've still got two eyes that still work. There's some redness in your left eye. That's due to pressure that's built up around the cornea. I'm going to prescribe some eye drops for you to use twice a day for a week. They'll keep infection out, plus they'll take away the redness. They'll sting some, but they'll get the job done. You can get them here or pick 'em up at the drugstore. There's one refill." Dr. Hollis told Mama, "I'd like to see her again in one week to check that eye."

"Yes, Dr. Hollis. And we'll get the drops here." Mama decided. "That way, we don't have to wait on your mother to go to the drugstore." She turned to Dr. Hollis and told him, "Thank you so much for helping my baby. She could have lost that eye."

"She'll be fine, Mrs. Lowry. You might want to bathe that eye with some Epsom salt, using just a little in warm water. Put a bath cloth in the solution, wring it out, and put it to her eye for about ten minutes at a time. Do this every day until the redness is gone. And you, young lady." He laughed. "You stay clear of flying rocks, especially the ones that hit you in the head, you hear!"

Mama called a taxi, and we waited in the *colored* waiting room. There was another man in the room also. I wondered what would happen if we went to the *white* waiting room. *Had anybody ever done it?* I wondered. I wanted to ask Mama, but from asking other insignificant questions, as she'd once said of my questions, I knew to keep my thoughts to myself.

The taxi (Frog) pulled up into the back of the office area. Mama helped me stand, though I probably I could have done it all by myself. I waved to the nurse, and she waved back; she was nice. She'd seemed hurt because of where Mama and I had been sitting, waiting for our taxicab. I wondered how much longer things would be this way. I'd ask Mother. But would she know?

"Well, Frog, my granddaughter almost left us today!" Mama told him again the story.

"Yeah," Frog replied in all innocence. "Where'd she go?"

"No, I mean she almost got killed. Yeah, a rock hit her in the head. The doctor said if it had been the least bit further over, it would have killed her. But isn't God good? He spared my baby's life!" She clapped her hands.

"Yes, m'am," Frog agreed.

After several more twists and turns, Frog pulled up in front of our house. The meter had $1.25 on it. He told Mama, "Just give me a dollar, Miz Lara."

"Low-ry-ry," I wanted to correct him.

"Do the little girl need help?" he asked.

"No, thank you, Frog, she'll be fine. I'm gonna get her in the house and into bed. She was almost killed today, you know."

"Yes, m'am, you told me she was. I sure do hope she go do all right."

"Well, that's mighty nice of you to say, Frog. Mighty nice. Doris, say thank you to Mr. Frog. He's a mighty nice man."

"Thank you, Mr. Frog." I obeyed.

"Yes, m'am," he answered. If a frog had come and gotten beside him, you wouldn't have known who was which.

When we pulled in front of the house, Mr. Frog blurted out, "Let me know if you need me tomorrow."

"All right," Mama said, "but I don't know whether Doris is going to school tomorrow. I might keep her out another day."

"Yes, m'am, I don't blame you," Frog replied. "She might not even be feeling like going."

"I'll be okay," I put in. "I just need some sleep and food."

"Oh, she's feeling better all right." Mama laughed. "She mentioned food."

"She sho' did," Frog agreed. "I believe she go be needin' a taxi-cab tomorrow after all."

When A Cousin Owns the Heart

THE BOYS DESCENDED IN OUR elementary school subtly, quietly taking seats in the back. They stood with the boys at short recess, playing the games boys play: marbles and cards and softball. At lunch, they sat at the boys's end of the table and took big bites of food that they chewed with their mouths slightly closed. I could see it all as I sat with the girls at our end of the table.

In class, the new boys answered questions with seeming ease about the presidents when we studied history, about number facts in math, and about the eight parts of speech during grammar—my favorite. Mrs. Edwards had said their names when she introduced them to our class: "Class," she'd said in her best teacher voice—encouraging—I don't take mess, "Students, I'd like you to meet Alvin and Michael Fisher. They're cousins, and they come to us from Greenwood, North Carolina. I want you to make them feel welcome. Now, say good morning."

We obeyed. "Good morning."

Michael and Alvin, not knowing what to do, just stood with blank expressions like question marks. Then Mrs. Edwards assigned a buddy to each boy, someone to help them learn the ropes. She picked Nate and Sonny Boy. Then, "Boys"—she nodded with her head—"you may take these seats back here." She walked them over as all of our heads followed. "I'll issue your tests in a while. Make sure you cover them."

Michael and Alvin nodded, saying, "Yes, m'am."

In the days to come, the boys settled in well and became perfect fits. They made 100s on our weekly spelling tests, 95s on history, 97s on grammar, and 96s on math. These numbers would often change, but when report cards went out, Michael and Alvin always had made straight A's in every subject, just like my sister. The novelty of these cousins continued well into the bitter winter months of my seventh grade year. Alvin was riding his blue boy's bike down Stampton Street at the exact time I was coming out of the big church on the corner. (Sister and I always referred to Zion that way.) We'd been to a wedding, and I was all dressed up in my Easter dress.

My hair was loose, slick, fluffy, hanging on either shoulder. We'd been to a wedding. Trying my best to look cute, knowing he was in the street below (I was at the top of the stairs.) I gave my head a little girly shake. It was just enough to make Alvin almost lose his balance and go falling to the sidewalk. I pretended I didn't see him and watched him, his mouth hanging open before, looking up at me. He stared for the longest time before riding off. I wondered what he was thinking, what was going through his mind. I would never know.

Our seventh grade year got closer and closer to its end. I knew those eight parts of speech like the back of my hand, what made a complete sentence, and how to tell one from a simple one, could rattle out science and math facts, and even knew about different continents, countries, and cultures. It was April, time to start thinking about May, when we'd have the school social. Already I was imagining Alvin and me (him in a blue suit and white shirt, me in my blue Easter dress) out there on the gym dance floor doing "The Twist." If he would ask me to dance, I'd jump!

Sure enough, we had our social, May 15, on a Friday night. By this time, Alvin and I were an item. I knew this because we stood together under the big tree every morning while waiting for the bell to ring. We just talked and hit each other on the arm. We'd glance over at each other and smile. We'd kick up the red dust under our feet and sheepishly giggle. Silly, silly, yes! When the eight o'clock bell would ring, we'd walk to our first class together in no rush. We tried passing notes, but when Mrs. Shaffer read one I'd written out aloud, our writing careers were over—just like that!

He had my phone number, and I had his, but Mama had said I couldn't talk to boys on the phone, and Alvin's mom wouldn't let him call up girls. We couldn't even sneak. So I had no way to tell that the two cute cousins wouldn't be at my school the next year. I didn't know that they were moving back to their old school and their old friends. I couldn't know that when I dressed on the first day of school next year, wearing the pretty dress I'd picked out with Alvin taking a front seat in my mind, what awaited me. I simply couldn't wait for him to see me, walking across the school yard, feeling like royalty.

Riding with a neighborhood teacher and getting to school earlier, I ran down to stand under "our tree." I wanted to be there, waiting when he got off the bus! I waited and waited. No Alvin. No Michael. *Maybe they missed the bus*, I reasoned as I walked, dazed, into school. They could have overslept. Perhaps they forgot to set their alarm clocks. I'd had all these things to happen to me over the years.

But that didn't happen to these boys. I found out the following week when they didn't show up. I must have been a pretty pitiful sight because Libby, a girl who'd had very little to say to me in the past, ran over in a puff. "Doris," she announced, a half-smile on her face, "Alvin and Michael moved back to North Carolina over the summer!" My face must have fallen flat on the floor and hard at that. I found myself fighting tears. I drifted through the first day of school day in a funk, thinking about what Libby had told me.

So Alvin, with his cute self, was gone! *Back to North Carolina.* I'd never see him anymore. My eleven-year-old heart crashed into a wall and shattered into tiny little pieces and went all over. I went from class to class, remembering where Alvin used to sit. For a whole week, I did this. By that Friday, while preparing myself to take that weekly spelling test, I noticed the desk where Alvin used to sit. There was the cutest boy sitting in it, Alexander Wallace.

Seventh grade was looking better all the time!

The Fight after School

THE RIFT HAD BEEN FESTERING since the first day of school. She'd said something first, something ugly, something I hadn't actually heard, but word had come. But the message got to me, second-hand, carried by the classroom troublemaker, none other than Cindy Lou. She came running up to me at the first of short recess, out of breath. "Doris." She panted, "Cindy Lou says she'll be waiting for you after school!"

"I'm not scared of Cindy Lou." I lied, hoping my nerves didn't surface.

"You should of heard what she said about Miss Nellie. She even talked about Miss Venie, who sure would get her," she added, looking at me intently to see if I was buying the bull.

The afternoon ticked by slowly then speeded up so fast, too fast. The announcements came on, but for the first time, I missed them, even the part about the book fair coming next week. I had to find out from Sherlene who was talking to Ruth about it, which book she had hoped to buy. "What are you going to do?" Shirlene, a quiet type ran up to me and asked. She waited for an answer; I had none. "What are you going to do?" The question again. This time, the anger that had been rising up to the edge all day spilled over, like water does when it gets too hot in a covered pot.

"Tell her I'm waiting in the back of the school!" The girl took off running. A crowd was gathering like rainclouds before a storm. I looked around for the duty teachers, but they hadn't come out yet. I trembled and looked around nervously. I saw red, as I thought about all the awful stuff Cindy Lou had said about Mother and Mama. My anger festered, growing to its boiling point. I glanced up to see my opponent slithering down the red dirt hill. She looked like a snake wearing a plaid dress.

I was ready, hot and heavy, so mad I was seeing double, triple even. Word must have reached Cindy Lou, for she came bounding down the hill. I slung my book satchel to the ground and lit into Cindy Lou. I was so fast with the push, it got her off balance. She almost fell backward. Quick, pent up with anger propelled me to hit her, raising both fists. I rolled her into the ground and pushed her into the waiting puddle of drying red mud. I grabbed her by her sweater and yanked her upright, just to slap her across the face.

"Don't nobody talk about my folks!" I blurted out, punching her upper arm. I kicked her leg as hard as I could, so angry I barely heard the teachers' voices over my classmates. "Girls! Girls! Stop this instant." One grabbed me and the other, Cindy Lou. Then to the jeering crowd, glad I had beaten the would-be bully.

"All of you children, get out of here now and go home, or you'll be in trouble, too." The crowds distributed quickly.

It was Mrs. Pelham who escorted Cindy Lou and me up to the long corridor to the principal's office. The walk proved scary. *What would Mr. Land do?* I wondered. I had missed the bus. How would I get home? The question that occupied my mind. Mr. Land called Mama first. "Mrs. Lowry," he said in a dignified voice, "this is Mr. Land from Edgefield Elementary School. I'm calling to let you know Doris has been fighting. The punishment for this is three days suspension, which both girls will get. They can make up any missed work."

Mrs. Law said she'll bring Doris home with her. Mrs. Law, the secretary, lived right across the street from us. I looked at Cindy Lou as Mr. Land found her number in the school information file and called her mother with the same message, just changing the name. I looked over at Cindy Lou. Her dress was torn in places. Her legs were caked with drying mud; her arms had scratches on them, and her nose still dripped blood. I wondered what fate awaited me at home. After all, both Mama and Mother had wanted Sister and me to stay out of trouble. Yet this was different. Though they had told us that words could do no damage, Cindy Lou's words had been hurtful and had dishonored both women. I was left with but one choice: fight!

When I walked into the house that day, Mama was waiting with cookies and milk, and a strap, which she did not use right then, anyway. She held out the food to me. "Hungry, girl?" she asked, eyeing the caked mud on my dress and shoes.

"Yes, m'am." I smiled.

"You must be with the day you've had down there fighting! What do you think your punishment ought to be?" She smiled, her half-smile then winked at me.

"She said bad things about you and Mother." I sobbed, tears flowing like a faucet. "She had no right to talk about y'all. You never bothered her or her family!" I was sobbing nonstop now, and I could not stop myself. The tension of the whole year erupted, boiling over like a volcano.

I just knew Mama was going to whip me with that black belt. She'd certainly used it before. But she simply put the belt back into the drawer. "You say Cindy Lou had a bloody nose?" she asked, a hint of a smile forming on her lips.

How did she know? I hadn't told her, I didn't think. Mr. Land hadn't. Maybe, Mrs. Law had when she dropped me off. Anyway, Mama sounded proud, as if to hint "I'm glad you beat her a_ _!" She looked me up and down. "These three days, you're out, you're gonna clean this house room to room. You're gonna start in the kitchen. I want you to take everything out of the cabinets and wash them down. Then change the linen on all the beds. Sweep everything down and dust." She kept on belting out orders. I was tired already. She stopped suddenly, gave me a sharp look, and said, "So you gave her a bloody nose?" A mischievous smile formed and slid across her lips, just as Mother drove up the drive way, so surprised to get the news that her daughter had been fighting and had actually won.

The Mad Dog Down Our Way

I T WAS AN EARLY SPRING morning. I awakened to the usual: dishes banging on the kitchen table, Mama singing, "What a Friend We Have in Jesus," Mother pattering down the hall, her bedroom shoes flopping.

I sat up in bed and tried to rub the sleep out of my eyes, but with no luck, for it was still there.

I yawned, stretched, and yawned again. What was that smell, that awful smell? *It's your breath!* that voice inside my head chimed out.

"That's your conscience," Mother had once told me. "It's God's help in telling us right from wrong," she had explained. She always knew how to make hard stuff simple.

I shook Sister, my hand over my mouth. "You awake?" I asked her, holding back a yawn.

"No!" she snapped. She must have had a bad dream.

"Girls," Mother called, "time to get up! Wash faces and hands, brush teeth, make your bed, and…" she stopped short. Mama burst in the back door just as we were entering the kitchen. Sweat was beading up on her forehead.

"We've got to call the police! There's a mad dog out there on the sidewalk!" She panted, mopping her forehead.

"A mad dog?" Mother responded, tenderly putting her hand on my shoulder.

We filed out on the back porch to get a look and saw a big brown dog. He looked like he was trying to run up the street, when all of a sudden, he'd run the other way. He kept doing this over and over, like in slow motion at first, then going faster. A bloody, beige mixture slid out of each corner of his mouth. His tongue hung strangely over to one side, and it dangled as he moved.

We could hear the guttural sounds coming from his throat, sort of like a car trying to start on a cold, winter morning.

We saw his eyes, hot-looking and blazing red, that shone through the new morning light. His mouth fell open, showing his teeth covered with the bloody pus-like film, sort of like the wolf in *Little Red Riding Hood*. That dog looked scary. Even his coat was ugly now. The brown that probably had once looked like a forest ground now looked just like mud on a bleak winter day.

Mother and Mama talked in whispers, like the mad dog might hear what they were saying.

"We'll call the police who'll contact the dogcatcher. He'll call Animal Control, I imagine," Mother commented. "Now, girls, come on in and get washed up and dressed. You've still got school, you know." She laughed.

We came off the porch, all except Mama who stayed to keep her eye on the dog. Mother got the phone book and called the police once she had the number.

In a manner of minutes, two police cars came rolling into the street where the dog was. He was still having those fits, rolling over and over as if trying to scratch his back.

I was dressed, with the exception of getting my hair fixed. Mama usually did it, but not this morning. She had more important stuff to do, like looking at a mad dog foaming at the mouth and rolling over, rolling over.

"Mother"—I tugged at her dress—"will you please do my hair?"

"In a minute, honey." She was trying to hear the talk going on between Mama and the officer, still sitting in his car. The blue light was still going round.

"Come on, you child." Mother directed. "And bring the Vaseline."

Oh, no, I thought, *not the Vaseline. Mother puts too much on my hair.*

"Let's go out on the porch," she suggested, "where the light's better." Sister came out, her hair ready in a bouncy ponytail.

"Will you make me a ponytail like Sister's?" I asked.

"Not this morning," Mother answered, lowering my head into position with her hand.

"I'm making you two plaits. Okay?" I wore two plaits every day to school. Sometimes they came loose, and Brenda would plait them back, hurting me on purpose. Sometimes Willie Strong pulled one or the other hard so it would hurt the longest time. I only bit back the tears and told him, "You're gonna get yours, Willie Strong," knowing full well it would never happen.

Mother patted down Sister's hair, encouraging her, "Vera, you've really gotten good at doing your own hair. Miss Doris should be starting doing hers soon. Right, Miss Doris?" She laughed as she tied the narrow bows on the ends of my plaits.

"Right, Mother, dear." I grinned.

The dogcatcher was putting a wire-like noose around the mad dog's neck. Mama stood outside, talking to the police, all were wearing big padded mats over their uniforms. The dog was pulling against the noose, seemingly pulling tighter the harder it was pulled. I thought he must not feel the tugs so enraged was he.

We watched as the dogcatcher pulled and tugged and loaded the mad dog into the back of the screened truck. There was a wire muzzled on the dog's mouth, but still the bloody, pus-like liquid seeped from around it. We could hear its muffled growls as he was being put into the truck and even once in.

"What are they going to do with the dog?" I asked Mother.

"They'll put him to sleep," she said. "Killing him gently where it won't hurt him a bit."

"*Wow!*" It's all I could say.

"Now, you two, have a great day and be good."

"Yes, m'am," Sister and I said at the same time. We grabbed our satchels and headed out the front door. I looked back and saw Mama still talking to the policeman. The dogcatcher was spraying the sidewalk with something green.

"Bye, Mama!" I called, startling the men. Mama waved. Sister waved.

I couldn't wait to get to school to tell my friends. As we stood in our usual spot under the big green tree, I puffed, "Guess what, y'all, there was a mad dog on our street this morning. Bloody stuff was coming out of his mouth, and his eyes were all red and bulging out like his tongue. He was making a strange sound and moving all funny like."

I was talking so fast I got out of breath. They looked at me, eyes wide in disbelief or shock. "A mad dog with bloody stuff coming out of his mouth all read and red." Delilah mocked. "What's a mad dog, anyway?"

"It's too early for dogs. They don't come around till the afternoon."

"Yeah, Doris, where this dog come from? Whose is it? What's his name?" The questions were coming fast. They were Brenda's. She hardly ever talked. I had no answers for her. I wondered what she wondered.

"I think you're fooling us," Lula Hopkins declared as we edged up to the door. I resigned to the fact that nobody had, nor would, believe my story—only the people who had actually seen the mad dog.

I really didn't care. I'd seen for myself the poor pitiful spirit of a dog gone mad. *Just like that of a real person*, I thought.

Chasing the Rainbow's Colors

SISTER AND I HAD BEEN waiting all Saturday morning looking at the telephone and waiting for it to ring. We waited and watched *Mighty Mouse* save the day and Sister paint her nails. Mama was dusting, and Mother sorting clothes. We made our beds and pretended not to be anxious. Daddy wouldn't lie, would he? He would wire the child support money like he'd promised to. After all, Friday was yesterday, the day he got paid. He always sent a wire by Western Union late Friday afternoon, unless Mary Mason got to him first. She was Daddy's woman and had been running his show for years, and Mother knew it too.

But Mother was no saint either, for her man came by every Friday night, married as he was. They met at the Elk's Club on Saturday evenings. When I should have been asleep, my eleven-year-old ears were wide awake listening to them talk in the living room. Finally, at about one-fifteen, the lady called, telling she had a wire from Detroit. Sister and I wore shorts, bearing this hot July day. Mama was in a house dress, and Mother, her favorite summer sundress.

After leaving Western Union, we headed over to the recently built Hardee's to get late lunch. Mother had given a dollar each to Sister and me. Oh, boy, a whole dollar to spend anyway we wanted to. Sister was saving hers, she announced as we neared Hardee's.

"I'm buying a hot dog and a Coke," I bolted out like I'd never had food.

We pulled into the parking lot, filling up with cars. Mother opened the door on her side. "Don't take too long, Doris, and come straight back after you get your food," she cautioned.

I shook my head and hopped up to the counter. Oh, but if I didn't feel like a big girl with that whole dollar in my hand! I was grinning ear to ear just like a piece of corn. The red-faced, smirking white man drawled over the counter, "Yep? What do you need, girl?"

I remembered my manners. "May I please have a hot dog and a Coke, sir? Oh, and here's my dollar!" I smiled and held it up. I watched him as he turned even redder than he was—his ears, nose, forehead. I thought his teeth and tongue must even be red, maybe even his teeth. He glared at me. But I just smiled and looked up at him. He was quiet, but I felt that he was thinking, "*What will I say to this* **colored** *girl.*"

Finally, I found where my tongue had been hiding and pulled it up to surface level. "I'd like a hot dog and a Coke, and some French fries too, if I have enough." I waved my dollar bill.

"You got 'nuff for the dog and the Coke, but that's all. And," he added slowly like it suddenly hurt to talk, "I can sell to you, but only if you go 'round to the back!"

Something on the inside of me changed. I didn't know what or how or even why. I just knew that I would no longer see the world filled with lollipops and rainbows and kittens. I would see my first holes filled with mud and trenches filled with muddy water and hungry children who cried because they were afraid of when tomorrow came; they'd be hungry again. I walked around to the back, like the white man had said, proud to have my own dollar, but broken because my pride had melted and was gone. I gave him my money, took my food, and threw it into the trash.

I was trying frantically to think what I'd tell Mother when she asked where my food was.

"You didn't eat it all?" she asked.

I just nodded. For many weeks, the words of that man would haunt me, and with no one to tell but Donna, my doll, and Anna Lee, my best friend. Donna had listened as she always did; Anna Lee had roared, "Oh, Doris, how could you even take that food? Go 'round the back! Who did he think you were? A slave?" She was hot and heavy mad.

"More like an indentured servant!" I laughed, playing off what Mr. Heath had taught us.

Prejudice wouldn't meet me again until years later when I was in college—an innocent, pure, unassuming freshman. I walked reverently in the annual Blue Line with the rest of the students to the big corner church. The minister, southern, white, had taken to his text from the Book of John. His words focused on Christian love. He reminded us that we must love each other as Christ had loved us. His words had sung true; they reminded me to love my current roommate who had no love for me (I later changed roommates, making all concerned happier). I was thinking about his message, and quietly talking with Jean when this man approached us and snarled, "Y'all go to your own church next Sunday! Don't come back here! We don't want you."

We four black girls were shaken, our eyes wide, our mouths open. We just stood there in a speechless daze, unable to move or speak. "I'm gonna tell my grandmother about this!" I told the three miffed girls, and I did. Mama was furious at the man's words and actions. She told the lady for whom she had worked, and she alerted the pastor who had heard similar reports about this man. Evidently, he had a record for this kind of thing, doing it every year.

The man was taken off the church membership book, his membership denounced. He was banned from the church permanently. I asked myself, "Why must there be prejudice in the world? Why can't people love each other with no boundaries or restrictions or even limits?"

That Sunday, I had traveled back to the Saturday when we went to Hardee's, of the red-faced man and his hateful heart-pounding words, "I can sell to you if you go 'round to the back." Had he been implying that I wasn't good enough to be sold to, like white people in the front? He might as well had the signs up displaying those forbidden words: *colored* and *white*.

Memories are pictures of past events, sometimes pleasant, sometimes unpleasant. Most of mine are favorable, happy, rainbow-colored. But the truth doesn't always come to light, and remember, if nothing else, the rainbow has no shadows or black stripes.

Those Boys Who Begged

THE FRONT DOORBELL RANG OUT its eight chimes. I always thought it was the beginning of a symphony. Mama went to the door to see two boys about my age, brothers, standing there. One of them spoke, "We don' mean to bother you, lady, but does you have some food we can git? We real hungry." I hung behind Mama, holding on to her apron tie, wondering what she'd do.

She stood there, looking over her glasses at them. "Nellie, Nellie," she summoned Mother from the back room. Mother came out, a question mark in her eyes.

"These boys say they're hungry. What do you want to do?"

"Find them plates, I guess. We have plenty left from dinner." Mother smiled, opening the door. "Come in, boys. What are your names?"

The taller boy spoke. "My name Jerome. This here, Jesse Lee. He my brother."

I was standing there, listening, looking, taking it all in. The boys were tattered in their clothing, and the heels on their shoes have holes in the bottom. They seemed to be nice, though. "Come on in the kitchen while I fix your plates," Mama directed. "You boys have to bring these plates back tomorrow, you hear?"

"Yes, m'am," they echoed at the same time, glancing up at her.

She spooned huge portions of chicken parts, rice and gravy, green peas, greens, sweet potatoes, and huge slices of cake. She filled good glasses with sweat tea, then piled the plates into a brown paper bag. She'd wrapped everything in with paper followed by aluminum foil. She put a piece of foil over the tops of each glass.

"We sho' do thank you, Lady," Jerome told Mama, taking the bag and one of the glasses.

"Doesn't your mama cook for you?" I blurted out.

"Doris!" mother exclaimed, giving me the eye. I knew what that meant: Shut your mouth, now!

Jerome answered sadly, "Our mama, she dead. Been a year now. We live wid our pa, but he have to work and don' have no time to cook for us." Jessie never said his grade. He just hung his head. Mother didn't press. "Thank you for dis food. We knows it go be good," grinned Jessie Lee as they headed toward the living room. "Yes, m'am," Jerome added, "it do look real good!" They left.

The next day, near dinnertime, the brothers returned. Jerome carried a brown bag, and Jessie Lee, the two glasses. "We didn' wash 'em cause our pa ain't had no money," Jerome told us. "He go pay it today when he get his check. Here. That food sho' was good!" He handed her the bag, and Jessie Lee put the glasses on the table.

"Thank you," she told them. Then, "What do you boys want to be when you grow up?"

"I want to be a doctor," Jerome beamed.

"I go be a fireman," Jessie Lee quipped.

"That's real nice," Mama told them, encouraging the brothers. "You keep going, and you'll get there," she added. She put the crusty plates in the sink followed by the glasses, each holding a bit of yesterday's tea.

"Well, thank you, again, m' am," Jerome said. Jessie Lee followed his cue.

"You're more than welcome." Mama patted each boy on the back, and Sister, Mama, and I watched them walk away, back to their world.

We were never to see them again but, at certain times, wondered about those boys. Were they eating healthy meals every day? And was their father paying the light bill? Did they live out their dreams becoming that doctor, that fireman? I never knew, though one day, I saw a boy out the corner of my eye down the street who looked just like Jerome. The clothes were still tattered, but they were bigger, and the shoes looked worn, like they might have holes in the soles. And the side of the face looked quite familiar. I said nothing as I passed quickly by, not to rouse attention. I only hoped his present condition along with his brother's had gotten better, that he and his brother, Jessie Lee, were eating better and had lights in their home. I only hoped but had no obvious way of ever knowing.

The Graduation High-Heel Shoes

T HERE SURELY WAS SOMETHING WICKED about June that made us children mischievous. Mama had warned me, "Doris, that tree in Anna Lee's yard was *not* put there for you to climb! You hear?"

Oh, I had heard all right. But trees were *made* for climbing. And that tree in Anna Lee's yard was no different. Only Miss Wilcox, the lady who lived across from Anna Lee, was watching and would surely tell Mama what she saw in the tree.

And then when Anna Lee's cousin Trish came down with her Aunt Ida from High Point, North Carolina, we all seemed in for it. There was not only the tree with that unforeseen sign saying, "Do Not Climb" but also the box in Mother's closet containing those high heel shoes—the ones she'd told us children to stay away from.

Well, I don't know which voice did the whispering that it was all right to pull the box out, but suddenly, we girls while pretending to be graduating from high school, had just the right shoes for the occasion—high heels, Mother's high heels.

Now Mother had given me permission to play using her *old* shoes. But these were her good shoes, the ones she wore to church, on special occasions, and other affairs. They were *not* to be played with. And here I was on the corner, with the box, passing out high heel shoes—Mother's to be exact.

We girls paraded back and forth, back and forth, back and forth all morning in the June heat, pompously marching up and down the sideways—supposedly auditorium aisles—all morning. In fact, we marched until morning melted into early afternoon, then to midafternoon, then to late afternoon. Time for Mother to come home from teaching in the Veteran's program, a fact my fun had made me forget for the moment.

Our graduation gowns were towels we'd sneaked out of the bathroom. We also used them to wipe the sweat that steamed down our faces. Just as we were getting ready to sing another round of "Pomp and Circumstances," Mother's 1957 Fairlane Ford slid around the corner full speed ahead. Evidently, she had spotted *her* shoes on *our* feet.

I sort of felt that June sun grow a little hotter, as I imagined what was on the way. Was Mother going to get me right here, out in the open, for everybody to watch?

Mother brought the car to the edge of the sidewalk where we were. Normally, she would have said something to her child standing out in the heat with her friends all around. Not today. She had her black book bag in one hand, and she slammed the car door shut with the other. "Doris Amurr." Uh-oh! She'd called me by both my names. That meant war, and I was on the wrong side.

She strutted by us, steaming, and not from the intense June heat either, but from sheer anger brought on by her baby daughter whom she loved just this morning. She must have been mad, for she slammed the door when she went in, which was a big no-no in our house. She came back out, quickly, like she'd never gone in the first place.

She said not a word but lashed out at us in all directions, slashing arms and legs and even sometimes faces.

She had Mama's thick black leather belt that she had used on me just that one time when I had pushed Sister down the Helms' front steps. The Helms lived in the house across from us. There was a mother, father, a big sister three ages up from Sister, and a brother who was Sister's age. In fact, they were in the same grade and same classes. Sister said Jerry could have been smart, but he played around too much.

Anyway, that belt was coming down hard in all directions, getting one of us, sometimes two, sometimes three, and even four every time. There was a tangle of legs and arms and fingers trying to shield against the thrashes, but absolutely to no avail. Mother was experienced in whippings; she'd learned from the very best: Mama.

We didn't know what to do. We couldn't run with those high heels on. And if we could have, where would we have run to?

The squeals made us sound like barnyard pigs in a pen waiting desperately to be fed that awful slop. Mother whipped and whipped, using that black leather belt until she was completely out of breath. She'd stop, then start up again, refreshed, renewed, ready to whip some more.

All of a sudden, she stopped. No more lashings. The whipping was over, had ended. "Doris Amurr, Anna Lee, and your visiting cousin, all three of you girls know better than to play in my good dress shoes! Those shoes cost money, good, hard-earned money. I work hard for my money, even in the summertime. Now what do you have to say for yourselves?" She waited.

"Sorry, Mother, I'll never do that again," I told her, fighting back the tears.

"I'm sorry, Mrs. Ezell. My mother would be awfully mad at me if she knew what I'd done. Please forgive me," Anna Lee pleaded.

"Mrs. Ezell, I'm sorry I played in your good shoes," Trish pleaded. "I'll never ever do that again. I promise."

"Come here, you three." Mother opened her arms, smiling down at us. "You know I love you. Now come on in the house and get some ice cream. It's hot out here. It'll cool you down."

"Yes, m'am!" the three of us answered in one big voice, suddenly healed from our much-deserved whipping.

I knew I'd never look at high heels with the same eyes ever again.

Rose Marie's Secret Situation

I WILL ALWAYS REMEMBER AND WONDER about Rose Marie's words in the letter that she wrote to me:

Dear Doris,

I've left home, probably for good. I'm living up here. And Doris, I'm not ever coming back.

Love, Your good friend,
Rose Marie Jones

She had written it the last summer she came down to her aunt and uncle's house. We were very good friends.

Her words had left me to wonder about some things, like where was up here? Was it a place, a house, a city, a town, or even another state? And why wasn't she ever coming back? Had something so terrible, so absolutely devastating, happened that she couldn't bear the thought of venturing back here? If so, what was it? What on earth had happened?

I wondered about it for the longest time. Many nights, I lay awake asking, "What had happened to Rose Marie?" Where on earth had it happened? Had she been so scared, so devastated, so fearful that she'd left reality and gone insane, out of her mind? For wasn't that the saying now, 'That poor girl's done lost her mind!'?"

Mama said it happened because of "some old pair of britches." I had heard her talking to Mrs. Harris one morning when I was supposed to have been outside playing. Mrs. Harris had walked up bringing a bag of okra from her garden. The two were talking on the sidewalk; the news hot and inviting. Of course, I told Anna Lee what her letter had said, and she started to wonder, too.

Then one summer day, I was helping Mama pick okra in her garden. I heard singing coming from across the street. Since it sounded like a child's voice, I being nosey, ran to see whose it was. To my surprise, it was Rose Marie, my long-lost friend who'd left last year and written me a letter saying she was never coming back.

"Rose Marie, you're back!" I yelped, happy as a clam to see my friend again. "But you said you were never coming back. Remember?" I reminded her.

She was quiet for a time. Then she said, "Yeah, I remember. But I don't think I'm supposed to tell."

Now I really wanted to know what this was all about she'd been talking about. A secret something that she couldn't tell. What would have happened if she had? I'd had secrets before, and of course, I'd told. I just couldn't keep them all to myself. Like having my boyfriend, Alvin Fisher. Even he didn't know about it. Yet why did he think I was looking at him, laughing all the time I was looking? Because it was a certain day of the week? Or because I had on a blue dress?

The days went on. Spring turned into summer; soon the leaves would be turning colors and falling off the trees. Then the days would grow colder; finally, it would start all over.

It was summer. The days were so hot, they could grow blisters on your bare skin if you didn't watch out. Rose Marie was back, and she came outside, wearing what looked like a new shorts set—I couldn't remember ever seeing it before. She simply said, tears in her voice, "Doris, he's still bothering me at night. It's gotten worse."

Immediately, questions began inside my head. *Who? Bothers how? Bothers who? Bothers what? What do you mean?* I was looking at her hard, woefully.

Tears started to mount up in her eyes. "He comes in my room at night and makes me, he makes me, oh, Doris, it's so awful, awful..."

she couldn't talk for crying. "He makes me do things, terrible things!" She sobbed.

Not knowing what to do or say, I knew a hug always helped me. So I put my arms around her, letting her cry into them all she wanted to. When she was spent, I told her forcefully, "You've got to tell somebody. Your mother, my mother, the preacher, somebody, Rose Marie. And you've got to do it right away. He can't get away with hurting you like this anymore."

"You're right. It's been going on for too long."

I gave her another hug. "Thanks for listening, Doris, for being my friend," she said as she walked back across the street.

Rose Marie and I were never to speak of the incident she'd shared with me anymore that summer. But the shame in her eyes let me know the abuse was still taking place.

I should have told Mother what she'd told me. I really regretted not having told when a few years later, I read a headline in the paper: "Local Girl Stabs Dad to Death: Molestation Suspected."

I knew right away who was involved and what the case had been about, but just a little too late to act.

Our Friend, Dash, the Dog

ANNA LEE AND I COULD hear the licks as we walked up the sidewalk. We heard his cries, his moans, low, muffled. We knew what was happening. Mr. Tucker was beating Dash again, poor innocent Dash.

Dash was a light-colored furry German Shepherd who loved licking my face, and who I loved having him lick my face, though Mama didn't. "That'll give you ringworms," she said when she found out. "Yes, m'am." I'd lied. I knew I'd welcome Dash's licks the next time they came.

"We've got to do something," I said.

"Yeah." She shook her head, agreeing. "But what?" We walked on up the street, thinking, wondering, hearing the licks and cries continue until they just stopped.

Seconds later, we saw Mrs. Tucker drive by in his white Cadillac, a fancy straw hat on his head. We heard the rattle of Dash's leash coming up behind us. He panted in his friendly way as he ran up to us.

"Hi, Dash!" I squealed. "How are you?" I gave him a big hug. Anna Lee repeated. Dash gave us each big sloppy kisses as if to say "Thanks for being my friend." We hugged him with all the love we had in our hearts.

Anna Lee and I were playing in her yard one day with Dash. He was chasing us, around and around. I never saw the big brown pile Dash had left on the ground; in fact, I didn't know it was there until I went slip sliding through, smearing it all over my spanking white sneaker. "Dash!" I squealed out in alarm. "Look what you did!" I just knew Mama would get mad at me when she saw my shoe, not white, but brown!

With it being summer, Mama was up earlier than usual to work in her garden. Mother was teaching the veterans in the army's program, so Sister and I were on our own. We read, looked at TV, did our chores, and were off—I went to Anna Lee's and got Dash, and Sister went to Lois's house.

Doris with Dash

The days were long, and the weeks appeared longer. It seemed that school would never open again. I even missed homework, lessons, even those mean old teachers who paddled kids for no real reason.

One morning, I awakened to hear Dash's crying. But there was something strange about it, something that said trouble. I quickly dressed and headed down to Anna Lee's, forgetting to eat my corn-flakes already poured into the bowl.

I could hear Dash yowling as I hurried past his house. What on earth was wrong? I was in a panic when Anna Lee came to her door. "What's wrong?" Her eyes were two big question marks. Tears cautioned her. "Come on, I'll ask Mommy if I can go to your house." She schemed.

Her mother was humming and seemed to be in a good mood. She just shook her head and reminded her not to stay too long, wearing her welcome out. I meant to ask Mama how somebody could wear a person's welcome out. I asked Sister first, who had just given me a sharp answer, "Oh, Doris, that's so dumb!" I forgot about asking Mama.

Anna Lee got the whole story as we walked down Miller Street. The closer we got to Dash's house, the more those strange sounds came out. "I see what you mean, Doris," Anna Lee said. "I hope poor Dash is okay."

"So do I."

The morning melted into afternoon, and Dash's moans got no better. They seemed worse by the time Anna Lee left. They went on and on, the rest of the day, it seemed, until they simply suddenly stopped. I called Anna Lee on the telephone, chattering my five-minute time limit. I told her how I didn't hear Dash moaning anymore when just earlier he had just been moaning his little heart out. "What do you think could've happened?" I asked.

"I don't know." She panted. "But there's one thing for sure. We've got to find out!"

"But how?" I asked. "How can we find out? I mean, do we go knock on his door and just ask, 'What's wrong with Dash? Why is he moaning?' He's never done that before!"

"I suppose we should," she said after thinking the matter over. "But Doris, I'm scared!" She admitted.

"Me too, but Anna Lee, we've got to do it!"

"Yeah, you're right," is all she said.

We were walking over to his house when we saw Mr. Tucker coming out, carrying a blanket. It was plain to see that Dash was on the inside. Yet we still didn't know what was going on.

It wasn't until the next day I found out. Mama, perspiring from working in her garden, found me on the side porch playing with my doll, came up to me and said, tears streaming down her face, "Doris, Dash is dead. He died yesterday."

She gave me a big hug and kiss. Later on, I told Anna Lee. We both hugged and cried all for our dog Dash. But we knew in our girls' hearts we would always want to know, "Did Dash die from the natural causes or from those awful, unlucky licks thrown by his master, mean old Mr. Tucker?"

First Sunday, August, Big Meetin' at Saint Luke

I REMEMBER IT LIKE YESTERDAY'S RAINSTORM that lasted most of the day. So did this church service. It was good, don't mind me, just long. And was it ever hot that day with only the paper fans and a slight wind that eased in with the flies through the open window near the front. There had been talk of getting air conditioning put in, but so far, that's all it had been—talk. I mopped the sweat that was rolling down my face with my hand. The collar on my dress was all wet.

The church grew quiet for a while. Then a man's robust voice lined a hymn, which meant he called out loud the words of each line in the song, and the choir sang them, then the next line until he'd called all the lines, and the choir had sung all of them.

An older man we knew as Mr. Quincy started to shout in his peculiar way. He started at the back of the church, ran up that aisle, and when he got to the end, he stopped and jumped up and down, up and down. Then he ran back down the same aisle, stood at the other end, and jumped up and down, and up and down. He was really feeling the spirit, as Mama would have said.

Along with Mr. Quincy and the choir was a fat lady in the front of the church who stood up and shouted, shouted, shouted with both arms flailing the air so hard that her broad-rim fancy hat went flying off. One of the ushers had to get it before it got trampled. One lady was shouting in the choir, and she got so spirit-filled that her breast jumped out of her dress. She just kept on singing and shouting, grabbed her breast and pushed it back down in her dress, and went on singing and clapping her hands like nothing had happened.

The whole congregation, Mother and Mama included, were feeling the spirit, for everyone was singing and clapping and patting their feet to the beat of whatever song was being sung.

Oh, it was a sight, looking across that church, seeing all the ladies in their wide-rim hats and floral dresses fluttering like flowers in the wind, and the men folk all in their blue or black Sunday suits.

Just as the song reached its climax, in walked the preacher, slowly, sure of himself like he was the Holy Spirit in person. He raised his arms, which seemed to caress the entire congregation, still humming and patting their feet.

His arms still stretched out as if he was reaching for the sky, he boomed in a mighty voice as large as the church, "Let the Church say Amen!" And everybody said together, "Amen."

He next exploded, I mean exploded, into his text about the resurrection of Jesus Christ, and how He died to save your sins and my sins. At certain times, his voice got so low, I could barely hear it; at other times, it boomed like thunder filling up my eardrums.

His short prayer ended up being a semilong sermon, which started into a few words that grew longer and longer and longer and longer even still. His sermon, though sounding good, talking about the same whoremongers Mama had said were going to Satan; only she'd said the H word. Mama probably could have been a preacher herself, knowing about the whoremongers who were all headed for H.

Mama became the preacher herself, preaching to Mother the mornings after she came home from the Elk's Club. She went every Saturday night with her two lady friends. (They met up with their guys once there.) They'd party until the Elk's Club closed. That's what Mama had told Mrs. Helms. I was listening to them talk; though, I was supposed to have been outside playing.

The pastor finally brought his sermon to a close by opening the doors of the church. I looked back but never saw the doors open. Besides, Mama gave me a quick pinch, bent down, and whispered in my ear, "If you turn around just one more time in this church, you know what you're gonna get when I get you home!" I knew exactly what she meant. The doors of the church would just have to open without my seeing them do it. I would ask Mama about those doors when we got home.

The choir sang the closing hymn. The pastor said the closing prayer, almost as long as the sermon had been. He then dismissed us to the kitchen where lunch was being served. Mama and Mother had packed some food in the trunk of the car, just in case.

"Let's see what's down there to eat," Mother suggested. "Besides, I'd like to see some of the people here." We walked through some large doors that led to some stairs. Maybe these doors were the ones the pastor had spoken about opening. The aroma of food met my nostrils and made me even hungrier than I was.

Two ladies dressed all in white came up to us as we neared the kitchen. "Come on in and help yourselves to anything you see down here," one of them said. "There's chicken, rice and gravy, green peas, candied yams, greens, mashed potatoes, macaroni and cheese, potato salad, broccoli casserole, all kinds of pies and cakes and drinks."

"Y'all, help yourselves. Get some of everything. There's plenty. And take some home with you!" She looked at Sister and me, hard. "My, my, what pretty little girls these are! What's your names, children?" the lady asked.

"My name is Laveria Frannett Ezell," Sister told her. "People call me Vera. My sister calls me that: Sister." I giggled. "And my name's Doris Amurr Ezell, and people call me Doris," I said.

"Well, you sure are pretty, both of you is. What grade you in?"

"I just finished seventh grade," Sister said, smiling. "I'll be in seventh grade in September."

"And I'll be in sixth grade when school starts in September. I just finished fifth grade," I offered, proud, proud, proud!

"Well, isn't that nice? You're smart girls," the lady told us. "Y'all stay in school. Get as much learning as you kin. I didn't get to go no further than seventh grade in school. But I'm going back. I'm in night school now. I'll get my diploma in June. I'm going to try to go to college after that if the good Lord's willing."

"That'll be really nice," Mother encouraged her. "You keep going until you have all the education you can get. I want my girls here to go all the way."

The lady thanked Mother, beaming as she walked on to help someone else.

She had fixed plates for the four of us. She's put some of everything on each. Mine was so loaded, the juices were seeping over the side of the plate.

Another lady came up to us as we sat eating at the long covered table, "Hello," she said cheerfully, "you girls have on some mighty pretty little dresses. Where'd you get them from?"

"My daddy sent them to us from where he works and lives from Detroit, Michigan. He sends us a box pretty often," I added.

"Well, isn't that nice? Your daddy certainly does have good taste in clothes," she added.

"Yes, m'am," Sister agreed. I nodded, agreeing.

"This food surely is so good," I told the lady in white standing next to me.

"Well, I'm sure glad you like it, hun," she said. "A lot of ladies had their hands in preparing this food, not just one. It was a joint effort, a joint effort," she repeated herself for emphasis.

"Girls," a man wearing a navy blue suit, said, "always obey your parents. They'll always tell you what's true. They ain't never lie to you."

"Yes, sir," Sister and I said at the same time. He was right too. They had no reason to lie to us. They never had, either.

"And always love them," he went on. "'Cause they they the ones who go love you. They the ones who go put clothes on your back, food on your table. Yes, girls, they sho' is the ones. And always love God." He ended his minisermon.

"Yes, sir," Sister and I said at the same time.

Saint Luke had been some spectacle that hot summer day. We'd heard good singing, seen a different kind of exercise with the shouting, heard a rip-roaring sermon and a prayer that was close to another sermon in the making. We had eaten good home cooking in a variety of foods that smelled good and tasted even better. We had met people who had said nice things that encouraged Sister and me to be good children. Oh, yes, it had been quite the special day, and certainly one I couldn't wait to get back to tell Anne Lee all about.

Donna, My Last Christmas Doll

I HANDED MOTHER MY CHRISTMAS LIST. It had two items on it: an Elvis Presley record and a Debutante Dolly doll. Both forbidden. For one, Negroes weren't supposed to like Elvis Presley because of something he supposedly said, and two, I was in the seventh grade. My friends would have a field day if they knew I still played with dolls.

"What are you going to do with a doll?" Mother asked, trying to shame me. "After all, you're getting to be a big girl."

"Yes, m'am, I know, but Anna Lee's getting a doll," I offered.

"And what grade is she?" she'd asked, looking over her glasses.

"Fifth grade. But we can't play dolls if we both don't have one. I really want that doll for Christmas, Mother, and the record. That's all I want!"

Nothing else was said about my Christmas list, but on Christmas morning, there she was, standing beside the Christmas tree, dressed in her blue velvet dress, white socks, and black patent leather shoes. She also had a second outfit, an evening gown—a long, flowing one made of net and lace. Beside her was my Elvis record. "Oh!" I picked up my doll and squealed, "Oh, she's beautiful! She's beautiful!" I couldn't wait to dress, eat, and head down to Anna Lee's with one of my treasures.

I pranced down Miller Street, swishing my ponytail and carrying my new doll like a child. I was so proud. I had gotten the doll, the record, two games, a rocking chair, and some clothes. Daddy had sent Sister and me a box from Detroit containing *two* dresses a piece, car coats, and knee-high socks! I named my doll Donna, and I carried her into Anna Lee's house with a big girl's pride, like she was the only doll on our block.

"Oh! She's so pretty. What's her name?" Anna Lee asked.

"Her name's Donna," I yelped joyfully.

"Come and see Frances, my new doll," she said as she led us to their living room. Their tree glowed with tinsel and lights. There stood Frances, a doll the same height as Donna. Frances wore a red-checkered pinafore dress, white lace trim, white socks, and black patent leather shoes.

I could tell Donna and Frances were going to be good friends, just like their mothers. They made small talk, getting to know each other until it was time for us to leave. Donna was a walking doll, so I let her walk slowly beside me down Miller Street, home. She was the kind of doll you put in your bedroom in a corner to look at. Donna stood in the corner of Sister and my room, looking as pretty in her blue velveteen dress. When one of my friends from school came over, she was put in the closet, kept out of sight. After all, she was still my secret doll, my last doll. Nobody should know she even existed.

My fun with Donna grew. I couldn't wait to get home from school to have my snack and talk with her. This continued until one day when I was in seventh grade, I came home relishing from the happenings of my school day. Mrs. Lanthroup, my English teacher, had read us a wonderful poem called "The Raggedy Man." She had put so much expression in reading it. I felt I knew the character, saw the holes in his pants and shoes.

I was ready to tell her how Mr. Shaw, my science teacher, had made me stand in the corner, holding a stack of heavy books. All I'd been doing was whispering to Patricia while he talked about how germs are passed from one person to another. But Donna was gone. I bounded into the kitchen where Mama was washing dishes. I was frantic! "Mama, my doll's not there. She was there when I left for school…" I couldn't finish because I burst into tears. Finally, "Where is she? Where's Donna?"

Mama hugged me and tenderly, softly, said, "Doris, you're in seventh grade. Too big for dolls. Don't you think it's time you passed your doll on to some little child who doesn't have one?"

Sister, Doll Donna, and Doris
Christmas, 1959

I wanted to scream. "No! She's my doll, for always. I'll always have her!" I sensed Mama had given her away. And all I said was, "Yes, m'am."

I missed Donna. True, I was in seventh grade. True, I was getting older. True, it was time for Donna to take her presence to some other little girl, to be there when she cried or had a secret to share. To be there, waiting for school to let out when she learned all the happenings that day, good or bad. To be there, like she had been for me when Daddy's child support Western Union money order had come. Sister's and my joy would be so high, like fluffy clouds up in the sky. To even be there when on some Saturdays, we'd wait anxiously, pretending not to be waiting by doing some unusual task—looking in the closet or through the drawers or kitchen cabinet, thinking about that money. I wondered about the girl who was now Donna's mama.

136

How did she look? How old was she? Was she nice? Where did she go to school? Did she have a boyfriend?

I missed Donna, her clear skin, rosy cheeks, and deep dimples. I missed her lips pulled into a bright smile that never left her face. I missed her perfectly painted fingernails, all ten of them displayed on outstretched, reaching hands.

Time passed, giving me many birthdays and many grade advances. I grew taller, and my feet got bigger. I went down one dress size, and though he didn't know it, Alexander was now my real, official boyfriend. Even when I was standing in my college graduation gown, proud, ready to teach seventh graders, I looked around at the corner where Donna used to live. I remembered her and all the happiness she'd given me and thought about how I'd never see her again or even get her back. But one fact still rings forever true: I'll always love and remember Donna, the last doll I ever got for Christmas.

The Monster Who Came
to Visit and Stayed

IT CREPT INTO OUR HOME, like a wily thief looking for what he'd steal first. It knew where Mama's room was, going straight there, bypassing mine, to first steal her memory. Of how to put on shoes, what day it was, where she'd put her false teeth last night. It made her forget about time: she was going to bed when I was getting up. About place, she walked uptown one day and could not find her way back home. About people, she called Tina, Doris, Doris, Tina and herself, Nellie Mae. It made her forget to be hungry: she simply stopped eating for a time, then for days.

It took away her ability to be rational, and she would often laugh out loud in church—during silent prayer, making even the preacher jump. This monster had to have been ugly and vicious and calculating and downright mean. Who else would, could attack an elderly woman who had once been so pleasant, strong, independent, and nice, becoming just the complete opposite? No one or nothing else but a monster. One with no imagination, green in color, and sharp, sharp teeth that badly needed brushing.

This monster was void of several things, like love and compassion. It didn't even like itself. It hated sunsets and springtime, forgot how to have fun, and often ran away from home. It rambled through the cabinets during the night and fussed on Saturdays when I was sleeping in. The monster sometimes sang, though its voice had long since been gone. It took long walks that got himself lost. He forgot to talk on the telephone but often talked to dead friends and relatives now up in heaven. The monster did things that confused her, like medicine times and eating times and even sleeping times. Sometimes when I was going to bed, Mama would be getting out of bed, getting ready for the new day. "Mama, it's night. Don't you see that street-light?" I'd pointed through the blinds.

"No, you child, that's the sun. See God's sun! It's time to go. We're gonna be late!"

Sometimes, this interplay would last for hours. The next morning, I would be dragging from lack of sleep and Mama, well, Mama would be pumped up! One morning as I was driving to work, sleepy, fatigued, ready for bed, I swerved over into the next lane, meeting a tractor trailer truck head on. I prayed, "Dear Lord, please spare my life!" From nowhere, an unseen hand had reached out through the air or sky and pushed me back over into my lane. No other cars were out there that morning. I was safe! I chattered and trembled most of the morning. It didn't dawn on me until I was driving home. I had been nearly killed that day. Only a miracle, an honest-to-goodness, real miracle, had saved my life.

JUMPING AHEAD IN YEARS

The Autobiography of My Left Hand
My left hand, see it hanging here,
Looking just a little queer?
From wrist down to the fingertips,
It curls, it slinks, it dives, it dips!
It's great for when I want to lay
My head on it to think or pray.
On my wrist, two terrific scars
Look just like ladders stretching up to Mars.
(They're really what the surgeon made—
Young Dr. Jeremiah Slade.
He tried to make the hurting stop
And keep my hand out of this knot,
But it still looks just like a brown ball,
And it hasn't stopped aching at all.)
Now perhaps you've heard
Some pretty absurd
Tales about how my hand got this way.
Well, make no mistake,
My hand didn't break—
Here are the facts; please hear what I say:
I'll tell you the truth, no jive, no jokes.

When I was sixteen, I had a brain stroke.
It crippled me badly, and I couldn't walk.
It slurred my speech, oh, I could barely talk.
It twisted my mouth, disfiguring my face,
And for a teenager, that's a real disgrace!
I lay in a coma for thirteen days,
My limbs were mush; my brain in a purple haze,
The stroke wiped out my memory,
and it crossed my left eye,
It messed me sooo severely that I wanted to die,
And messed up I remained for a long, long time,

140

Until God stepped in and when He did,
He fixed my body and my mind body and my mind.

Yes, my left hand is a funny sort
It never does what left hands ought,
But something I recall a lot,
It's the only one I've got!
And since God made straight, strange, old and new,
And gave to all people different points of view,
To me, a strange one's better, y'all,
Than having no darn hand at all!

©Doris Ezell-SchmitzJ
2017

Looking at a Dream:
The Best Christmas Tree Ever

At Christmastime when I was growing up, what I remember well is the Christmas trees we had. They were always put in the picture window, no matter what they looked like. Like the tree that had some tinsel hanging down and six pitiful lights.

Another year, we had an artificial green tree that had the different colored-glass balls all over it. Still another year, our tree, green to start with, had so much artificial snow on it that it looked beige. The multicolored blinking lights saved it, however.

Our Christmas trees always had their own personalities, like that disaster that only had the tinsel hanging down and those six pitiful lights.

Yet in the legacy involving our Christmas trees is the one our cousin Annie gave our family that year when I was twelve. Annie, like I said, was our cousin. She was a nurse. She worked uptown for Dr. Denver, an old white man who'd always been that way—old.

Annie and her husband JD, who was a barber, lived in a white house across from ours. They didn't have any children, only lots of nephews who lived in the next town over.

In Dr. Denver's office was a beautiful silver white Christmas tree, decorated with glittering red balls and tinsel hanging down. There was an angel dressed in red and white, sitting on the top branch. She wore a golden crown on her head and held a golden *Bible* in her hands. She made the tree a pure deity, queen, a real princess.

When the office tree was to be taken out of the office around December 22, Dr. Denver gave it to Annie. They already had a tree; Annie asked Mama if we wanted it.

Her answer had been, "Gladly, Annie, money's a little tight this year, with Stanley being laid off and all." I'd been listening in at the door, hoping we would get the white beauty of that tree.

That same afternoon after JD came home, Annie had him go and pick up the tree. Mama already had swept from behind the couch and had pulled it out, making room for the tree.

Sister and I waited, peering through the picture window that sparkled from the Windex cleaning it had just gotten from Mama. We finally saw the truck turning on our street. We ran to the door to hold it open.

JD and two other men lifted and tugged and pulled until they had the tree standing upright and stately in the picture window.

All three of us were smiling, being really toothy. We thanked the men, and Sister and I boomed, "Merry Christmas and a Happy New Year."

Mama held the door for them. She smiled. "Thank you so much, and JD tell Annie thanks to her and Dr. Denver. I'll be over later with food for Boy." Boy was their dog, and they loved him like their child.

The men told us good-bye and left, with Mama still holding the door.

Sister and I simply adored that tree. We'd look at it for the longest times, not talking, just looking at the dream.

The rest of the holiday, we enjoyed that sight in the picture window. That year, I got a doll, some games, a view master, and a brand new coat. Sister got a typewriter and typing lessons, given every Saturday morning with Mrs. Myers as the typing teacher.

And perhaps, the best present of all had come in the form of a long-distance call from Detroit. It was Daddy.

"The strike ends the first of January of the next year," he'd told Mother. Money would be coming every Friday again without fail.

Something else too, the next time report cards came out, both Sister and I should have made all A's.

Vera and Doris cutting out paper dolls

Doris Is Ready To Sing
In The Children's Choir

Girls Dancing at School Social

About the Author

DORIS EZELL-SCHMITZ TAUGHT LANGUAGE ARTS at Chester Middle School for twenty-seven years and taught for one year at Lewisville High School and four years at Indian Land Middle School. She also taught for four years at Union County School District in Weddington, North Carolina. She also taught English at York Technical College in South Carolina. Doris has published two volumes of poetry, *A Teacher Testifies, a collection of poems centered around her teaching career and Beyond Superlatives: Encounters in Indonesia, storytelling poems that narrate adventures which took place during a five-week Fulbright-Hays study-travel grant.*

Doris was a featured reader at Spoleto Festival and MOJA Festival, both in Charleston, South Carolina. She has conducted poetry workshops in the local school district sponsored by the Rock Hill Arts Council. She has read in classrooms through the Reading Is Fundamental (RIF) Program.

Because of a brain stroke suffered fifty years ago, the fingers on her left hand are partially paralyzed. Doris considers this a help rather than a handicap. She sees sunshine, even on cloudy days. She is married to Jim, has two daughters, two granddaughters, and a toy Chihuahua, Cocoa Kennedi East. Doris resides in the house she grew in, some sixty-something years ago.